BLUE SKY LIGHTNING

BLUE SKY
LIGHTNING

*How To Survive And Thrive
When Life Blindsides You*

A TRUE, INSPIRATIONAL STORY BY

JEFF KUHN

LIONCREST
PUBLISHING

BLUE SKY LIGHTNING
How To Survive And Thrive When Life Blindsides You

ISBN   978-1-5445-1232-7 *Hardcover*
      978-1-5445-1231-0 *Paperback*
      978-1-5445-1230-3 *Ebook*

CONTENTS

ACKNOWLEDGMENTS

The first person I want to thank is my big brother, Rick Kuhn. Without his tremendous support, there would be no *Blue Sky Lightning* in print today. He believed in the project from the beginning and has stood by me, as he always does, through the long book-writing process. He took me to Chicago Cubs games at Wrigley Field when I was very young, and he has always been my best friend and trusted ally. He served in the United States Navy for twenty-five years and has spent the last twenty-five years taking care of my mom and dad while holding down a full-time management job. If anyone deserves to be called a hero, it is certainly Rick.

I also have to thank the trio of skilled surgeons who saved my life: Dr. John Hunt, Dr. Gary Purdue, and Dr. Rod Rohrich. All three are great human beings, in addition to being caring physicians. They treated me at the University of Texas Southwestern Medical Center in Dallas, Texas, which is home to more than ten thousand wonderful healthcare professionals. I owe tremendous thanks to so many of these gifted men and women. I spent most of my time at Parkland Hospital, but I had the opportunity to meet many individuals from the medical school and affiliated hospitals. Our country is blessed with hundreds of outstanding medical facilities, but I will always cast my vote for University of Texas medicine. Let's not forget the heroic men and women of the Dallas Fire Department who rescued and transported me safely and quickly to Parkland Hospital. They risk their lives every single day for all of us, and I wouldn't be alive to tell my story without their expertise and bravery. I wasn't born in Texas, but I did live there for ten years, and my beloved dog, Sparky, is a native Texan. God bless Texas!

I also want to thank my publishing team at Scribe Media in Austin, Texas, who guided me through the very complicated process of taking my story and turning it into a book: Katherine Sears, Scott Atkinson, John Mannion, JT McCormick, Tucker Max, and Zach Obront. Without all of them and everyone at Scribe Media, *Blue Sky Lightning* would still be just an idea. I also want to thank the incredible Dorie Clark for introducing me to Tucker Max and Scribe Media back in January 2018.

In addition, I want to thank New Trier High School in

Winnetka, Illinois, Dartmouth College, the Kellogg School of Management at Northwestern University, and the University of Southern California for giving me the finest education any person could hope to receive. I'm very proud to be a graduate of these world-class institutions of higher learning.

I'm very lucky to be from Chicago. There is no better city or group of people anywhere. We love our teams, win or lose, and Chicagoans all stick together. Anywhere you travel in the country, you always have a new friend if you meet someone from the Windy City. Chicago will always be home. A special thank-you to Anthony Rizzo (formerly of the Triple-A Tucson Padres) and the rest of the 2016 Cubs for making sure my brother and I (and Cub fans everywhere) were able to witness a World Series championship during our lifetimes.

My mom and dad play a big role in my story, and, of course, I have to thank them for giving me a happy, loving, and wonderful childhood. I could not have asked for better parents. We lived in the same home from the time I entered kindergarten to the year I enrolled at Northwestern University. The stability and care they gave me cannot be overstated. I love them both so much.

And, certainly, last but not least, I have to thank my wonderful wife of nineteen years, Gail, and my great son, Jeffrey Thomas (better known as "JT"). JT will be leaving for college next fall, and it's so hard to believe we're already at this point in his life. I feel like he was born yesterday, and I will be very proud to see him move on, but also incredibly sad his time at home has come to an end. The three of us have had great trips together from the time he entered our lives in 2001. I'm looking forward to all the new adventures that are coming in the years ahead.

First there was Rin Tin Tin. Then there was Lassie. Now, get ready for Sparky. Here we go...

FOREWORD

BY ROD J. ROHRICH, M.D.

Life has challenges and opportunities for everyone. The key in life is to take challenges and make opportunities, not only to make yourself better but to become a role model for others to be better each and every day. This is exactly what Jeff Kuhn's life has exemplified in his dramatic recovery from multiple life crises experienced by his life-threatening burns.

I had the opportunity and pleasure to treat Jeff at Parkland Memorial Hospital in Dallas, Texas, through some of those intense times during his treatment for severe burns. He demonstrated the ability of someone who never gave up, never hesitated from the moment his family was told he had only days, maybe hours, to live. His family did not give up on him; he did not give up on himself. He survived, and not only did he survive, he thrived. He has strived to become a role model for all of us and epitomizes the best of the best in the human spirit.

This passionate and compelling story of a tragedy turned to a life victory and lesson for all of us illustrates Jeff's incredible tenacity, hard work, focus, and ability to give back to others. It was a true honor to be his physician and it exemplifies the reason why we become physicians—to provide excellent healthcare to those who need it and to give back.

This book has taught me many lessons in life, including that of intense focus, never giving up, always having hope in spite of intense tragedy, and knowing that the most important thing in life is to look forward, never backward. That is the true human spirit, as in Jeff Kuhn's current life—to look to the horizon for positivity in life. Enjoy this book, as I have, in giving you hope and learning the lessons of life to help you become a better individual. Jeff Kuhn's book is all about living life with the cup always full!

Dr. Rod J. Rohrich is a plastic surgeon at Dallas Plastic Surgery Institute and former President of the American Society of Plastic Surgeons.

INTRODUCTION

WHEN LIGHTNING STRIKES

There is such a thing as Blue Sky Lightning. Actually, that's my term for it. Scientifically, it's known as "a bolt from the blue." This is what happens when lightning travels away from a thunderstorm instead of straight to the ground. Meteorologists have recorded lightning bolts striking as far as one hundred miles away from a storm. It's an incredibly rare occurrence. Compound that with the fact that getting struck by lightning is very rare—even in a storm. We don't hear about Blue Sky Lightning, or people getting struck by it, very often. It's about as unusual as it gets.

Yet Blue Sky Lightning strikes all the time, but in a different, more symbolic way. In my case, it even struck in the same place twice—at least that's how it seems.

When I was thirty-one, I woke up one day with 80 percent of my body covered in severe burns. Doctors told me I'd been in a medically induced coma for a month, ever since there was a fire at my home in Dallas. My condition was so bad that a priest had already given me my last rites.

As far as I knew, I'd gone to bed the night before after letting my yellow Labrador retriever, Sparky, go outside. Now, here I was. I spent the next two years going through seventeen major surgeries and intense physical therapy, making a recovery that shocked the doctors even more than it shocked me.

After my long, painful, but ultimately successful recovery, Blue Sky Lightning struck again.

I developed a neuromuscular disease that doctors could not accurately diagnose. All they could say for certain was that I was going to die, and that it would be slow and painful. Again, somehow, I survived—and learned to thrive.

My story may be extreme, but it's also something everyone can relate to. Life throws us these lightning bolts when we least expect them—whether they're something physical, mental, or emotional—and making it through often feels impossible.

I saw a psychiatrist on TV recently who had worked with

patients who'd gone through serious trauma, and she said something that has stuck with me: "Nobody makes it through life unscathed."

That's why I'm writing this book. None of us make it through unscathed. Lightning strikes us all. But not all of us make it through our trauma. This isn't just a book about being struck by lightning. This is a book about what happens afterward, about making it through. It's a book about survival.

I've met a lot of survivors. I've also met people who did not survive, whether that meant with their lives or coming out the other side with their emotions or mental well-being intact.

What I've learned is that you have to fight and know *how* to fight. In this book I'll be sharing two overarching lessons:

1. You are not alone.
2. You have the strength to make it through.

YOU ARE NOT ALONE

When you first experience trauma, it feels like you've been singled out. It's as though everybody else has gotten a free ride, and for some reason you've been picked by the cosmos to go through this incredibly bad event. You're scared. You're angry. You think, *Why me?*

That's how I thought. And one of the biggest lessons I learned—a lesson I want to share with you—is that everybody, at some point, is fighting a battle.

This might have been a more obvious lesson to me because I spent two months in a burn unit, a place full of people in bandages where there's often someone, somewhere, screaming in pain. But the lesson really came later, once I was out of the burn unit and in physical therapy. It was there that I saw so many other people with so many other problems. There were burn patients, cancer patients, and God knows how many other kinds of patients. And that was just in one rehab center. There were, I realized, millions of other people with millions of other problems out in the world.

It's important to realize this, because it's so easy to think about all the people who are not struggling. I've heard many people say to nurses or physical therapists, "You don't know what I've been through and you don't get it." But when you hear encouragement from someone who does get it—or even when you learn the hard lesson that, as bad as you have it, there are people who have been through the same thing or worse—then you realize you can't feel sorry for yourself. You stop thinking, *Why me?* You realize there are plenty of people who have had it worse than you, so you choose the option to be happy to be alive, keeping your head down and working that much harder.

Because of the severity of my burns and the long duration of my stay in the burn unit, I became something of a veteran burn victim. I earned a lot of respect from my fellow patients because so many of them would be in and out in a week, while I was stuck there for an indefinite period.

They would all ask me the same questions: "How did you get burned?" "How severe are your burns?" "How long have you been here?"

Without realizing it at the time, I was teaching them the first lesson: they weren't alone.

Inevitably, after those questions, there was always another one that followed: "How do I get through this?"

YOU HAVE THE STRENGTH TO MAKE IT THROUGH

Unlike me, most of the other burn patients came in conscious, and they were scared to death. All of a sudden, they were rolled into this burn unit and had no idea what was coming. I had to brace them.

I had one roommate for at least two weeks who came in

with third-degree chemical burns from his factory job. The burns went from the tops of his thighs to his feet. He was a young guy, probably about twenty-one, and was covered in tattoos. He was mad at the world. He yelled. He swore. He was rude to the nurses.

I tried to simmer him down, but he insisted on being angry.

As a burn patient, every day you get a bath...except it's not really a bath. What they call a bath is, technically, called debriding—a process of cutting off dead and dying flesh with a collection of razor blades, knives, tweezers, and scissors. It's beyond excruciating.

My roommate was having real trouble getting through it all. He was screaming, kicking the big metal bathing tub, and using profanity. He couldn't understand how I could make it through the daily pain.

"Look," I said. "You just have to realize they're not here to torture you. The only way to heal is to be debrided. They've got to get the dead skin off so you can heal and, yes, it's painful, and even though it feels like an eternity, it only lasts for an hour."

I reminded him that once he was done, he'd be wrapped in clean bandages and he'd be able to rest and the pain would subside. I reminded him that while he was being debrided, the nurses would change his bed, and he could always look forward to clean, fresh sheets waiting for him.

It didn't work.

"I'm not going to go anymore," he said. "I'm going to refuse."

I said, "Then you're not going to heal."

But even this didn't matter. "I can't get through the pain," he said.

I still don't know how I thought of what I said next. Maybe my dog, Sparky, was on my mind. But I said to him, "Okay, every time you are in excruciating pain, start barking like a dog."

"What?" he said.

"Seriously," I said. "When the pain gets bad, start barking."

The guy thought I was out of my mind. The next day, we took our "baths" at the same time, only separated by a large, white curtain.

He started doing his same old thing, kicking the tub, yelling profanities. So I barked.

My nurse, who knew me well at that point, asked me, "What are you doing?" I just held my finger to my lips.

All of a sudden, things on his side of the curtain went dead quiet. All of the screaming, yelling, and kicking just stopped. Then I barked some more—and he barked back.

He barked again, and even laughed, if only just a little. I barked again; he barked again. The nurses told us we were insane, but after we barked, he never made another peep.

Maybe the nurses were right. Maybe we were insane. It was certainly the craziest thing I'd ever thought of. But after that, he never complained again. He had been Mr. Tough Guy, but in the end, he turned into Mr. Polite. He was much nicer to the nurses and became a lovable guy. The "bark bonding" we shared helped us both.

Through first realizing he wasn't in this alone, and then being crazy and finding some humor, he found the strength he needed to make it through the most painful thing he'd ever experienced.

On the day of his discharge, he was wrapping up his stuff with his girlfriend and a nurse, and I heard him say, "God, I can't wait to get out of here. I never want to come back." He was the tough guy again.

The three of them left. Then, about ten seconds later, the door opened. He came back alone. He just looked at me. Then he said, "Jeff, I have to tell you something." He was staring at the floor, unable to meet my eyes. The tough-guy persona was completely absent. I could tell this was a side of himself he seldom, if ever, showed in his life.

"What?" I asked.

He said, "There's no way I could have made it through these two weeks without you. Thank you."

I'm tearing up while I write this, because I didn't realize at the time how much I'd helped him and what it meant to him—how important it was for him to find the strength to get through. No one wants to feel weak, but this was particularly true of him. He was a tough guy. Yet he needed to realize—in this case through a crazy coping mechanism: barking!—that he did have the strength to make it through.

You have that strength, too, even if you haven't found it yet. And with this book, we can find it together.

FINDING HOPE

To find strength you must have hope.

There are many situations that seem hopeless, but they aren't. You may be stripped of everything, but you can always have hope. In some situations, like the ones I've been in, there were points where the only thing I really had left to hang on to was hope.

The worst thing you can do is let yourself or someone you're trying to help lose all hope, because that's the last thing to go. After the fire, I wasn't able to move. I wasn't able to walk. I wasn't able to do a whole lot of things. But I was able to hope.

There is always hope. It may be small, but that small amount is all you need. You take that small amount and grab on, and it can get you through. It may take more than one day or a week. It took me more than two years of continuous hope and hard work after the fire.

Hope can require tremendous effort, but the work is always well worth it. Hope has given me twenty-five more years of the full use of my arms, eight more years with Sparky, and a whole new life.

NOT HOPING IS UNACCEPTABLE

Sometime during my first two months in the burn unit, the doctors came to see me and said, "Look, we just have to lay out some statistics for you here. Your arms and sides were badly burned. The odds of you being able to have full range of motion and full use of your arms again is pretty low."

I thought, *Wait a minute.* I said to them, "That is unacceptable. This is unacceptable to me."

They looked at me, and I saw that they were smiling. They laughed.

I said, "Why are you laughing?"

They said, "Because we want you to recover. We want to see you fight. You're showing us what you've got on the inside. There's a fire in there. We triggered the mechanism inside you that not everybody has."

They were talking about hope. I believe that everyone has it. Sometimes you just have to find it.

I found it despite some very bleak statistics. When the doctors told me it was unlikely I'd regain the full use of my arms, I told them to put a number on it, statistically. They looked at each other. Then they explained the surgeries I'd already had and the ones I would have to have just to give me a chance of getting my range of motion back. Even if those surgeries were successful, they said my chances of getting back the full use of both of my arms was probably between 7 and 10 percent.

I smiled. "As long as you're telling me it's not zero, I'm hearing 100 percent."

One year later, I was at the park doing chin-ups with Sparky by my side.

Like I said, you don't need much to start with.

GET FIRED UP

I have a fighting side and a good sense of humor. Together, they helped give me the motivation I needed to get through my recovery. Nothing motivates me more than when someone tells me that something is impossible. You have to find what motivates you. Think about the places you've yet to travel to that you'll see after your recovery. Think of the time you'll have with your friends and family. Whatever it is for you, find it and use it.

Mostly, you have to find it on your own. You're not going to have somebody walking along with you every step of the way like your own private motivational coach. Once I was out of the burn unit, it was just Sparky and me.

A lot of whatever you're going through is going to be painful. It's important to find ways to make it tolerable, even if you have to bark! In other words, be creative. Reward yourself along the way—go see a movie or dine at a new restaurant. Use the things you love to help you through.

I'M PROOF YOU CAN MAKE IT THROUGH

In fact, I'm proof twice over.

When I found out about my neuromuscular disease after I'd recovered from my burns, I couldn't believe it. How could something so traumatic be happening again? The pain was just as excruciating as the burn injuries. My muscles and nerves were self-destructing simultaneously.

I felt like I'd already climbed Mount Everest, planted my flag, and climbed down, only to have someone pat me on the back and say, "Guess what? You have to do it again."

And so all I could do was laugh and say, "I know how to do it."

The odds were once again not in my favor, but at that point I knew how to hope and fight. I knew I had the strength to overcome great difficulty. I had the roadmap of my past recovery tattooed in my brain. War had been declared again, and I was going to battle with everything I had.

THE ROADMAP OF THIS BOOK

That roadmap of recovery is what I'm going to share with you in this book. Each chapter will alternate between a different part of my story and the lessons learned along the way. I'm writing about this journey so that whatever you're going through now, we can do it together.

Like I said, you're not alone.

Chapter One

WHEN YOU'RE ALONE IN THE FIRE

When I was a little boy, I told my parents the first thing I would do when I had my own house was get a yellow Labrador retriever. My mom's best friend had a yellow Lab, Cinco, and I used to play with her all the time, but my parents wouldn't let me have a dog. They thought our street was too busy and might endanger our dog.

Instead, they got us a cat, Nikki.

Now, I loved our cat, but from then on I was dead set on having a dog. I knew I wanted a house someday, and I knew I wanted a female yellow Lab. Fast forward to 1987, and those goals hadn't changed. I was three years out of business school and buying my first home. Sure enough, three months after I closed on the home, just as I told my parents I would, I adopted my yellow Lab. I got Sparky.

Life was good. I was married, I had fantastic friends and a great job, and I owned my own home—it even had a nice backyard where I could watch a nine-week-old Sparky romp around.

Really, everything was perfect.

And then, it wasn't.

THE FIRE

Two years later, on October 14, 1989, I woke up in a fog. It was early Saturday morning. There was some light—just enough to see. The sun had just risen above the horizon.

There were some people around, and I remember thinking they looked like they were dressed as firemen. "We're here to help you," they told me. As it turned out, they *were* firemen. Two firemen from the Dallas Fire Department, to be exact.

I had been in a fire.

It was as though I was in a hazy dream. I was just watching. I would later learn I had been about as severely injured by burns as someone could possibly be, but at the time, I wasn't in pain—or perhaps the pain was so excruciating that I was beyond the threshold of feeling anything.

That brief moment of coming to was the first of only three things I can remember from that early morning.

The next was the jolt of the wheels on the stretcher as they loaded me into the back of an ambulance. I think that jolt brought me back into consciousness—and then I went back under.

The third and final thing I remember from that morning was opening my eyes and seeing trees fly by. I don't remember hearing anything inside the ambulance, not even the siren. It seemed like the driver was going one hundred miles an hour because the trees were going by so quickly. I looked away from the window and saw the paramedic, his face looking down at me.

"You're gonna be alright," he told me, and I went back out. I wouldn't be conscious again for another month.

LIFE BEFORE THE LIGHTNING

To this day, no one knows exactly what caused the fire that nearly ended my life. Sparky was the only eye witness, and she kept it all to herself. We did know pretty quickly that my wife and dog were safe. My wife was out of town, and Sparky, luckily, had been outside. My wife and I had been married for two years, and we had been enjoying a very normal life together. We had many friends and enjoyed traveling together.

As with many tragedies in life, there was no precedent for this one. I was a happy, successful young man with a good job, my own home, and a wife and a dog. The years had been good to me. Just five years before, I'd graduated from Northwestern University in Evanston, Illinois, with a graduate degree in business, and, by the time I had the house and Sparky, my student debt was paid off. I got a job with a commercial real estate developer and relocated to Dallas. It was a good time to be a developer in Texas. At that time, everybody there was building high rises. It was like a gold rush town, and I'd struck gold. Young people from all over the country were moving there, including some of my closest friends. It was an easy transition to a new and exciting city.

My goal was to be making $100,000 by the time I was thirty and to be a millionaire by thirty-five. I had big plans. There didn't seem to be any reason why that couldn't happen.

BLUE SKY LIGHTNING

The ambulance brought me to Parkland Hospital (part

of the much larger University of Texas Southwestern Medical Center), which has one of the best burn units in the country. This was lucky for me, because, normally, if you're burned on over 80 percent of your body, you do not survive. In fact, no one expected me to.

I was put into a medically induced coma for about a month to spare me the unbelievable amount of pain I would have experienced.

It wasn't until I woke up that I would learn everything in my life had changed. It would also be the first lesson in just how much life can change when you least expect it.

Blue Sky Lightning is the only way I can describe it. You can be standing outside on the nicest, clearest day in the world, and be hit by a bolt of lightning that's traveled from a storm more than one hundred miles away. That's how it felt when I woke up. My life, when I'd fallen asleep on one of those normal, uneventful nights at home, was like that perfect sunny day. There wasn't a cloud in sight, and yet somehow lightning still managed to strike.

I lost everything. My health was in jeopardy, and soon my money, my career, and my wife would be gone.

All I would have left would be a stack of bills, dozens of big problems...and Sparky.

But when I came out of the coma, I didn't even have my dog—they're not exactly welcome in a place that has to stay as clean as a burn unit. I was covered in bandages and learned that I'd already had two major surgeries, and my struggle was far from over. My recovery, during which so much more of my life would unravel, would be a two-year process involving an additional year of physical therapy and fifteen more surgeries.

As the fog in my brain cleared and I began that two-year journey, the doctors told me how lucky I was. I almost laughed. Lucky? How could anyone call this lucky? I didn't even have an idea of just how bleak things would get over the next two years, but this seemed bad enough.

Now, all these years later, I've learned that those doctors were more right than even they realized. It was a time of my life when I would learn major things about myself, my fellow burn victims, and the nature of life—what it takes to keep living, even during the bleakest of times.

Chapter Two

YOU FIND YOU'RE NOT ALONE

When the Dallas Fire Department paramedic in the ambulance told me, "You're gonna be alright," I believe my brain soaked it up. Somehow that thought stayed with me. On the brink of dying, I could have fallen one way or the other. Little things make a difference, and I'm sure those words are one of the things that helped tip me the right way. As I was about to be put into a coma from which the doctors did not expect me to wake up, those words stayed with me on some deep, subconscious level.

When I finally did come to after a month, I wasn't thinking about what the paramedic had said. Like lots of people who go through traumatic events—whether it's an illness, an injury, domestic abuse, or loss—I had a different attitude.

"I'm totally alone. I'm the only one going through something like this."

That was my mentality when I started the long process of recovery. It's not the same as feeling lonely. It's as if you're lost in the woods or floating in the middle of an ocean. You have to figure out how to handle the problem by yourself—there's no one else there to help you. Sometimes, you don't even feel like talking about your situation, because you can't imagine that anyone is going to understand.

Slowly, however, things in my life made me realize this wasn't really the case.

KEPT APART

Animals are just about the last thing anyone would allow into a burn unit. The staff knew how much I loved Sparky, but they firmly told me, "Look, you can have pictures of her, but there's no way we're letting you bring in a dog." After all, she could end up killing half the immunocompromised, infection-prone patients.

More burn victims die from infections than from the burns themselves. Your bandages are being constantly removed and replaced, and your body is covered in huge open wounds. Your immune system is almost nonexistent. A common cold could take you out.

So, a dog? No way.

It would have been easy to let that make me feel more alone. But I would sometimes return to that brief, foggy memory of the paramedic leaning over me, telling me, "You're gonna be alright." When I remembered that, I realized I wasn't alone. There was someone in my corner who had my back.

I also thought of *all* those people behind the masks. As the doctors, nurses, and staff talked to me, I realized there *were* people who cared about me and wanted to help me, even if I didn't know them. I realized that's the world we live in, one in which there are people out there just waiting to help you. When I started to notice other patients, I saw there were plenty of people in the same boat as I was.

There were times when I was lonely, but I realized I was not alone, even though it could seem otherwise. I started thinking, *I'm not alone, because there's a whole huge burn unit full of people fighting the same fight.*

That gave me a tremendous amount of strength, enough to begin what would end up being a very long battle. And it was good I realized it then, because as soon as I was conscious, the battle began. I was at war, and it was time to fight.

A WHOLE HOSPITAL, TOGETHER

As I described in the Introduction, every day in the burn unit, each patient had to undergo a process called "debriding," in which nurses use a combination of razor blades, tweezers, knives, and scissors to cut away what was either dead or about to die. They are literally cutting off pieces of you every day. It's called a "bath," but it's nothing like a bath. It's beyond excruciating. It's pure torture. You're in a large, stainless-steel tub, and it begins with the nurse rinsing you with warm water. When the debriding begins, the clear water turns dark red, and you watch as your own blood runs down the drain. You get used to this after a few days. Even when you weren't taking your "bath," you could hear the other patients moaning and screaming in pain from theirs. It sounds dismal, I know, and in a lot of ways it is, but it's also something that made me, strange as it sounds, feel better.

I knew I wasn't alone—not in the burn unit and not in my pain.

When something bad happens, it's easy to think you're the only one it's happened to. Seeing and hearing other patients made me remember that everyone has their burdens. We're all suffering. I might be in pain, but that didn't mean my pain was unique or that I alone had been singled out for this kind of misfortune.

And then, of course, there was the staff. The debriding might have been torture, but the nurses weren't torturers. They were helping us heal. It's hard to imagine someone choosing to work in a burn unit. It's a place of immense emotion and suffering. Many of the people who worked there weren't making a fortune at their jobs; they were there because they truly cared about what they were doing, and about the patients' well-being. I was impressed that the nurses and doctors didn't just come in to do their jobs—they also stopped by our beds to see how each of us was doing.

I knew the staff wasn't there to cure any loneliness the patients might feel. But they made us feel less alone, because someone actually *could* help us when we were lost in that forest or floating in that ocean.

Whether it's hospital staff or friends and loved ones, it is nice to know that somebody out there has got your back.

BATTLE SCARS

Something I experienced after leaving the hospital also helped me feel less alone.

I'd been surrounded by burn patients for a long time. When I got back into the "real world," I was worried what people would think of how I looked.

Over time, though, through different experiences and interactions with people, that worry lessened, and then disappeared altogether.

About eight years after my burn recovery had officially ended (1999), I was in Mexico on my second honeymoon. I was with my new wife, Gail, whom I had met in 1997. (She and I now have the world's greatest son—Jeffrey Thomas, or "JT." He just turned 17.) One day on the beach, I was playing volleyball and took my shirt off, playing in just my swim trunks. At the end of the game, I made a desperate dive for the ball, managing to touch it, but failing to hit it back over the net. Our team lost by one point.

Someone from my team came up to me after the game and said, "Dude, what happened?"

"I'm sorry," I told him. "I thought the ball was going to be in, and I was just trying to save it."

He looked at me, surprised. "I'm not talking about the game. I could care less. Look at your body—what the heck happened to you?"

"Oh yeah," I said. "That."

"Yeah, that. It had to be pretty major."

I told him my story, and all he could say was, "Wow. I can't believe you're alive."

We all have our battle scars. They might not be visible, like mine—maybe you've suffered emotional or verbal abuse. There could be no outward signs you've gone through something traumatic, although it's equally terrible. My battle scars are extremely visible. I am fortunate, though, since virtually all of them are hidden if I'm fully dressed.

And usually, I do keep them covered. In fact, this was the only time since the fire to this day that I've been out in public with my shirt off. I'm not self-conscious about my scars, it's just that they just tend to draw attention and I don't want to make anyone uncomfortable. But this was my honeymoon, I was feeling relaxed, and I thought, *Why not take my shirt off and get some sun?* Lots of people saw me, and this was the only guy who spoke up. He didn't make me feel like I should be ashamed. Instead, he was impressed. He wanted to hear my story.

What I've come to learn is that people are very understanding. Instead of saying, "Oh my God, I really don't want to look at that!" when someone sees my skin grafts, they're respectful. They want to know what happened and are glad I'm okay.

When I started dating again, I wondered what women

would think of me. My scars didn't bother me—they were signs that I had overcome something. I had expected to meet at least a few women who would say, "Look, I like you, but I can't deal with touching those skin grafts." But not a single one of them had the slightest negative reaction. Every woman I had a relationship with liked me for who I was.

All of this has taught me that, not only are we not alone, but that the vast majority of people out there are really good human beings. They'll be there for you, if you let them.

THE PARAMEDIC'S MESSAGE

Over time, those last words from the paramedic have come to have a deeper meaning for me.

When he told me, "You're gonna be alright," it was probably because he was trained to say that. But—and this is what has stuck with me—it's also human nature.

I find that encouraging.

If you were walking down the street and saw someone who was injured or beat up, you'd call an ambulance and wait with them. The first thing that would pop into your mind would be to tell them they're going to be alright, because you want them to be okay. You'd root for them.

You wouldn't look at another bystander and say, "This guy doesn't have a prayer." Every part of you would be pulling for him and hoping he made it.

The paramedic who was with me in the ambulance that day didn't know me personally. He does this for a living. I'm one of thousands of patients he's seen. But he was still pulling for me. I'm sure that later that day, he was thinking about me, saying to himself, "I hope that guy is doing alright."

Here's this stranger—not my mom, not my dad, not my best friend—who was rooting for me. If the roles were reversed, I would have been rooting for him. That's the nice thing about the way most of us are wired. We see someone in need and we want to do something about it, or, at the very least, we hope they'll be okay. We'll stay with them until the ambulance comes, we'll tell them they'll be alright, and we'll let them hold our hand if they need to.

The paramedic was the first person to help me understand I wasn't alone.

It's a lesson we all need to learn. Before anything else, realize that no matter how lonely you feel, no matter how alone you feel, you are not alone. There's a whole world out there pulling for you.

Chapter Three

———

WHEN DEATH
SEEMS INEVITABLE

When I was still in the hospital, it took time before I learned just what had happened to me.

When I came out of my coma, I was confused and groggy from all the meds I was on. I had no idea what had happened, and the doctors knew better than to overwhelm me with too much information. They explained I was in a hospital, that I'd had an accidental injury, and I was going to be fine. They kept telling me I was lucky, which seemed strange, given the circumstances—being in a hospital, covered in bandages. How could I possibly be lucky? Didn't they see how awful this all was? I could sense, as they told me all this, things weren't good.

When I was finally given the full story, I understood a lot more clearly why people kept telling me how lucky I was.

I found out that on the Saturday morning I arrived at the hospital, two of the best burn doctors from the University of Texas (Dr. John Hunt and Dr. Gary Purdue)—not to mention plenty of other hospital workers—spent the entire day just getting me stable. Their goal, essentially, was just to keep me from dying, and even that wasn't expected to be a long-term victory. About twelve hours after the accident, when my parents arrived at the hospital, the doctors told them, "Wednesday is about as long as we can envision him hanging in there."

In my condition, I was supposed to die. Death at that point wasn't a possibility. It was an inevitability.

LAST RITES

My parents are Roman Catholic (as am I) and very serious about their faith, so they went to look for a priest. My parents wanted to stay hopeful, but after listening to the doctors, they asked a priest to administer last rites. This way, when I passed, they would feel confident they had done the right thing for my soul.

When I think of this, I imagine the priest gowned up in hospital garb (good thing priests will do just about anything to administer last rites!) with just my mom, dad, and me in the room, while the priest rubbed the holy oil in the shape of a cross on my forehead. I say imagine, because even though I was there, I can't remember it. I was still in a coma, with no idea of what had happened to me. In fact, strange as it might seem, I was never told any specific details about that moment until recently. In all the years since it happened, I had never asked until the last time I met with my parents and I finally brought it up. They told me they believed there was no reason to tell me any sooner, since they believed it might be disturbing. I'm glad now that we've talked about it, but after all these years it still brings home just how close I was to death.

I didn't think it would bother me, since I'd already heard the doctors tell me how close to dying I was. But the mental image that came to me of the priest putting the holy oil on my forehead sent a chill up my spine. That's about as close to being gone as you can get; a priest won't administer last rites if everyone thinks you're going to pull through. Once they put that cross on your forehead, it's basically like saying, "We need to go pick out a coffin for this guy."

I've never met anyone else who's been given last rites and is alive to talk about it.

THE BURN UNIT

The first thing the average person might notice about a hospital's burn unit is the smell. But when I finally came out of my coma, I didn't even notice it. It turned out the fire had caused me to lose my sense of smell, which was lucky at the time. It meant I didn't have to deal with the odor of charred flesh and medical chemicals.

So for me, at least, it smelled fine. It also looked okay. Because of patients' compromised immune systems and the high risk of infection, the burn unit looks like a scientific laboratory. Doctors, nurses, and visitors have to wear special suits. It is immaculately clean. The patients are covered in clean, white bandages.

What I couldn't escape, however, was the noise.

There are probably some units in the hospital that are pretty quiet all the time. Burn units, on the other hand, are different. The only reason patients are there is because something incredibly terrible has happened to them.

The sounds of the burn unit are the sounds of pain. There's a great deal of screaming, crying, and yelling. There are quiet moments, but they only last until the next person gets their "bath" or is being rewrapped in bandages, or a new patient, unfamiliar with the excruciating pain of being burned, is wheeled in. Even with your door shut, you might not know exactly what's happening out there, but you can still hear the agony of the burn unit. For new arrivals, it was "welcome to the jungle."

This was where I would begin my new journey and, as I would learn in time, a new life.

HOW MY PARENTS HELPED ME SURVIVE

I can't imagine what my parents were going through at that time. But I know, whatever the outcome, they would have survived.

They are currently both in their mid-nineties—not something you often see with a married couple. Beyond that, it wasn't until recently they needed any outside help. Right up through their eighties and into their nineties, they were incredibly mobile. They did all of their grocery shopping, laundry, and house cleaning, and my dad still went to church every morning.

On the surface, they're funny, intelligent, and easygoing. They gave me a stable and happy childhood. We lived in the same house all through my youth, and when I went off to college, that house in Winnetka, Illinois, was still the home I came back to.

They're just good, happy-go-lucky people, but there's

a big fight inside of them that will rise to the occasion. That's why they're still around. They're fighters.

They passed their happy-go-lucky attitude on to me, but it wasn't until I was in the burn unit that I realized they'd passed their inner fight on to me as well.

A burn doctor I would later talk to noticed this. She considered the fact that my parents have lived so long to be part of what helped me survive my injuries. Making it into your nineties is partially due to genetics, but a lot of it has to do with mental fortitude and a strong survival instinct, as well as just being determined to live a good, full life and stay healthy.

It's not easy being in your nineties. You need help doing almost everything, and it's even harder for people like them, who had stayed so active for so long. Luckily, my parents have a good sense of humor about everything, including this. My mom often tells me, "Our goal was to live as long as we could. Well, now here we are; we've achieved it...and maybe checking out at eighty-five would have been a better idea."

I think that sense of humor helps you with the struggles in your life, and also helps you stay healthy. It's part of the inner fight. It's one of the best things they ever gave me, and I never realized it until I needed it.

When I started to recover from my injuries, one of my doctors, Dr. Rod Rohrich, told me, "I think your bizarre sense of humor is the reason you made it. You go into a surgery that's going to be six hours long telling jokes, and when you wake up in pain, you're still doing it. I think your saving grace was that you just found humor even in the toughest situations."

But that came later. No one was thinking that way when my parents were standing by my bedside. They hadn't come to cheer me up. They hadn't come to fight. They came to be with me as I died.

AGAINST ALL ODDS

After I received last rites, the hospital was essentially waiting for me to die. But they hadn't given up. That's not what they do in their profession. They continued to give me fluids and to treat my wounds. They still wanted to give me every possible shot at making it, even though the odds seemed like a trillion to one.

I was unconscious and hooked up to countless machines, and suddenly, something changed. Instead of going down or flatlining, the curves on the monitors were going up. This shouldn't have happened—I was about to check out. Of course, these were just small signs, but they meant that, against all odds, somehow, I was getting better.

The staff was pulling for me, but my unexpected improvement must have sent them scrambling. From maintaining me, all of a sudden, they were thinking, "If he's going to fight, we've got to dive in with him." They made a game plan. If I was going to fight, they not only had to fight alongside me, they had to do what it took to give me even more of a chance to survive. Without surgery, I wouldn't have made it. So, they figured out which area of my body they needed to administer a skin graft to first. They did surgeries they'd never thought they would have to perform—first one, then a second. All the time, unconscious, I kept slowly recovering.

COMEDIC MEDICINE

The surgeons who worked on me make me think of Hawkeye and Trapper from *M*A*S*H*, the hit TV series based on a medical team on the frontline during the Korean War. MASH stands for mobile army surgical hospital, and my wounds reminded my doctors of injuries they had seen during the Vietnam War. Hawkeye and Trapper were the best in their field and deadly serious about their work, but they were also comedians.

Hawkeye and Trapper, being in a war zone, saw many terrible injuries. My surgeons were in a similar situation. In their kind of work, where all you see are horrendous injuries, I think you need to have a good sense of humor and stay a little bit crazy in order to keep from going insane. Hawkeye and Trapper saved countless lives, but they spent their free time drinking homemade gin and playing practical jokes on the rest of the unit.

Knowing Dr. Hunt and Dr. Purdue, my own personal Hawkeye and Trapper, I'm sure they had that same sense of humor when they realized my vitals were improving. I can just see them looking at each other and saying something along the lines of, "I can't believe this guy is coming out of it. Now he's giving us more work to do! Two five-hour surgeries! Alright, here we go."

Knowing those guys the way I do, I'm pretty sure they wanted to meet me when I came out of everything. When I did, they told me, "We're still not sure how the heck you made it."

"Well, you saved me," I said.

"Yeah," they told me, "we helped."

It turns out I was lucky in several ways. I was the right age to survive these kinds of burns—my early thirties. If I had been younger than ten or older than fifty, as much as I might have wanted to survive, physically I wouldn't have been able to withstand the damage. I was also in very good physical condition, which was a tremendous help, the doctors said.

They kept asking questions about me and my lifestyle, trying to figure out just why I hadn't died and how they could still be conversing with me. When we talked, I would always joke around with them. And they said, "Okay, well, you've got a sense of humor. That must be it."

It wasn't the last time I'd hear that.

On a sad note, Dr. Purdue was killed by a drunk driver many years later, a terrible tragedy on so many levels. I wish I could have thanked him again, but I won't get the chance. May he rest in eternal peace. Dr. Hunt is still practicing medicine in Dallas, and I will make the trip to see him so I can thank him again for everything he did for me.

THE BOY IN THE RED WAGON

A sense of humor was important, but there were times, early on, when I realized that keeping a smile on my face was hard, if not impossible.

When I first came to after a month in the hospital, the doctors still weren't sure I was going to make it. There were two burn units: the main one, which housed the general population of patients, and the more intensive burn unit, where the patients had a long way to go before they were out of the woods, and they were monitored every second.

There were a lot of machines in the intensive care unit and very few beds. Mine was one of them.

The Dallas hospital, also a medical school, is a huge institution with over ten thousand employees serving an enormous number of patients. In our unit, however, there were only perhaps a dozen. One of the first I noticed was the patient in the room next to mine, a three-year-old boy.

His name was Eric, and he was adorable, with his brown hair and sweet smile. If the nurses doted on the rest of us, which they did, it was nothing compared to what this little guy got. The nurses would carefully put him in a red Radio Flyer wagon and take him on a short ride around our small unit, just to keep him entertained and get him out and about. Every day, I knew when he was coming, because I could hear the squeak of his wagon wheels approaching. I don't know why, but he would always tell the nurses "Stop!" when he got to my open door. Then, he'd say, "Hi, Jeff!" and I would say, "Hi, Eric!" and tell him it was great to see him.

For me, this was more than just being nice to a kid. I didn't have much interaction with people other than the nurses, and this small daily exchange with Eric meant a lot. I looked forward to saying hi to him. Seeing him made me feel good while I lay there, immobile and bandaged, and I thought, *I hope I make him feel good, too.* I listened for his wagon wheels every day.

One day, I told a nurse how much I liked his visits and asked how he had ended up there. That was when I learned something truly awful: many of the children in burn units are there because of abuse.

It turns out that one day, Eric's mother wasn't at home. Like many kids that age, he couldn't stop crying and whining. Her boyfriend got annoyed and filled the bathtub full of scalding water and dipped the boy into it. That's what had brought him here, with third-degree burns on his legs.

When I heard that, I wanted to collapse. Suddenly, I couldn't care less about myself. I had been recovering, learning about this new reality, but now my situation felt totally unimportant. I had wondered before how the doctors could tell me I was lucky, and I now knew my condition was nothing compared to what this little boy had experienced. I thought about how the boy's mother must feel. Mostly, though, I thought about this friendly little kid—how could this happen? How could anyone do this? I wanted to go strangle the boyfriend. I hope they threw him in jail, and if he's still alive, I hope he's still there.

Knowing what had happened to this little boy, and knowing that so many other children were suffering for similar reasons, was hard to take. Unfortunately, things got even worse.

One day, the wagon didn't come by.

Okay, I thought, *maybe he's got something to do today*. But then I didn't hear the wagon wheels the next day, either. After two days of not seeing Eric, I asked the nurse what was up. "This is two days in a row that I haven't seen him," I said, "and he stops by my door every day like clockwork."

"We didn't want to tell you," she began.

"Tell me what?"

"He passed away."

To this day, I still think about him. I know he's fine and in good hands now. But at the time, all I could think was if I could have rolled out of my bed and traded places with him, I would have. I was thirty-one years old, and still, hopefully, had a lot of life ahead of me. But I was thinking of what that little guy was going to miss. I'd had thirty good years already, and this kid had had almost nothing.

I'm writing this book to talk about the importance of fighting, about the strength that resides in all of us. But Eric's story is a grim reminder that there are times when keeping a positive attitude seems impossible. I went through a lot during that time, but of all the terrible things I saw in the unit, and all the terrible things that happened to me when I got out, that was the only thing that truly broke my heart.

Surviving is hard enough on its own. It's even harder because there are stories like this along the way. Not everybody makes it. That was what Eric taught me. It made me realize that those who are lucky, like me, have an obligation to ourselves and the ones we love to keep fighting, to take whatever chances we have, and fight for them.

And besides, as shocked and depressed as I was, I also knew that my little friend wouldn't want me to give up.

COUNTING ON YOURSELF

Someone who had read the article I wrote on LinkedIn about my recovery sent me a letter, telling me, "I respect what you went through, and your willpower and resilience. But you really downplayed the religious aspect of it. To me, your story is a miracle from God."

There's a reason I didn't insist on the role of God or religion in that article, and why I'm not doing it here. I agree that God definitely played a part in my recovery, but I just can't see myself as someone special that God selected. I saw a lot of people who were even more deserving of a miracle than I was and didn't get one. Eric is on top of the list.

I don't know why that little guy wasn't saved, and I don't know why I was. I'm no saint. I'm not a prophet. If miracles are going to be handed out, he should have gotten one.

There are reasons for what happened, and maybe I'll know them someday. But what I do know is you can count on yourself and your mental fortitude, because really, that's all you've got to count on. The rest isn't really up to you. That can sound depressing, knowing you're not in total control, but it also makes it essential to take control of the things you do have power over in whatever situation you're in. I was incredibly lucky, but if I hadn't fought, I wouldn't have made it through. You have to give yourself the best fighting chance you can.

I believe in prayer, but what my parents have always told me is that God may not answer your prayers the way you expect. It's a hard lesson to learn. So is the idea that your prayers might not be answered, and there may be a good reason for that, even if you can't understand it. I'm sure Eric's mother was praying like crazy for him.

When your prayers are answered, that doesn't mean everything becomes easy. I prayed to survive my injuries, and God answered my prayer. But He didn't come out of the clouds into my hospital room, wave a magic wand over me, and let me walk right out of bed. Maybe the answer to a prayer like mine is that God will give you the power to get through what you're facing. One thing I definitely believe: God will send the right people to assist you at just the right time.

Whether you're religious or not, ultimately, it still all comes down to you. You have to do your part of the work. You have to put up the fight yourself.

YOU ARE THE CEO OF YOUR RECOVERY

"Look," Dr. Purdue and Dr. Hunt told me. "You keep trying to give us all of the credit, which we appreciate, but really, over 90 percent of this is going to be you. You're going to have to get up and fight every single second of every single day, for quite a while. We won't always be there. Yes, we've done the surgeries, but we have to move on to other patients. Most of this is now on you. You are the CEO of your recovery."

I was about to move into the main burn unit, the place for people they think will make it. Death was looking less like a certainty.

"We've never seen anyone as badly burned as you live," they went on. "So, unfortunately, we don't have any advice for you. We can make some guesses, but, in the end, your recovery is going to come down to you and how you just tough it out."

When they moved me to the main burn unit, it should have seemed like a victory. But it wasn't a complete one. Just because I was in the main burn unit didn't mean I would necessarily survive.

I was still covered in burns. Death was still a possibility.

But death was no longer an inevitability. My prayers and my parents' had been answered. I had a chance. It turned out my fight had only just begun.

Chapter Four

YOUR FIGHT FOR LIFE IS AMAZING

One of the most important things my experience has taught me is it's hardwired into all of us that when your life is on the line, you are going to fight to the finish, even if it's with your last breath.

This sounds like something out of fiction, but it's absolutely true. I was unconscious for a month, but my body was present and my brain was still functioning. My brain and body had a consciousness higher than my own and knew I was in the fight of my life. I've learned that your brain and body will do everything in their power to survive. It's as if your system turns into a supercomputer to figure out billions of ways to get out of your situation, even if it seems hopeless.

Hopefully, you'll never be in a situation where you're scrambling to hang on and seconds count. But, if you are, your body and brain will rally and put up a world-class fight. All you have to do is join in. You may not win, but you will go down swinging. The fight for life is amazing.

DREAMLAND

When I say I was in a medically induced coma, it may bring to mind a state of complete unconsciousness, like you see in the movies. In my case, I wasn't completely out the entire time—just heavily (and I mean heavily) sedated. I had surgeries and visitors I don't remember to this day. But there are a few things I do remember from that time— other things I found out about after the fact. It was a very strange time, a time in my life I call "Dreamland."

CNN was kept on in my room twenty-four hours a day, to keep my brain stimulated. It's funny that, as out of it as I was, I remember major world events that happened then, like the earthquake during the World Series between Oakland and San Francisco, and the Berlin Wall being hammered down by a bunch of students.

Sometimes, when I could peer through the fog of all those drugs, I thought those stories were what I was actually experiencing. My best friend, Dick, came to visit me one day, and apparently we talked for a while. I don't remember a moment of it, but he said there were times when I was quite lucid...and times when I was a little on the crazy side. According to him, I didn't know why I was in the hospital, but I knew who he was and I could remember events from our childhood. Then, out of nowhere, I would tell him I was being held hostage in a foreign country and he had to contact the ambassador or the US government to tell them to come rescue me.

He didn't really know what to say to that (who could blame him?), so he just went along with it.

It was strange, but I can see the logic of what my brain was doing. I had to be kept still in order to heal, and so I was strapped down on the bed. I was hooked up to lots of different tubes. I couldn't move. Through all the morphine and Valium, and the lack of any physical stimulation while I just lay there, my brain was trying to put together just what the heck was going on. Being a hostage or a prisoner seems like a reasonable conclusion to make.

So, when I saw a familiar face, I asked him to rescue me. The poor guy. I can only imagine what he was thinking. Here I am one minute talking about childhood memories, and the next I'm a prisoner in Eastern Europe, plotting my daring escape. At least, in the long run, it's something we can look back on and laugh about now.

Dreamland is what it felt like. I was in some kind of dream state, punctuated by moments of vague consciousness. In a poem by Edgar Allan Poe, he describes Dreamland as a state of being on the edge, floating back and forth between life and death, not really sure which way to go.

A memory from that time is very vivid: I woke up in the dead of night. Everything was pitch black, except for the glow from the monitors and machines attached to me. I didn't know what they were; I was just in the dark surrounded by lights—red, yellow, and green. A TV was on, but I couldn't hear it. Through the window of my room, I could see an area with just one light at a desk, and someone sitting at it. Obviously, that person was a nurse, but in the moment I didn't make that connection. I didn't know anything, not even where I was.

Because of all the drugs I was taking, I wasn't scared. I remember saying to myself, "This is interesting. Where am I?" I wasn't in any pain. I felt like I was floating, just visiting the hospital, looking at these cool colored lights and noticing the person sitting at a desk.

If I could have known where I was and what had happened to me, I think I would have preferred to stay in Dreamland, because when I woke up again, this time for good, I would feel pain, and find out just how much more I had ahead of me.

SURVIVAL AUTOPILOT

What my body and brain were doing while I was in Dreamland was surviving. They were fighting the battle for me until I was ready to join the fight. What does this show us? It shows that fighting is an innate part of who we are. It's what our brains and bodies do. All we have to do is join in.

The doctors did everything they could to stabilize me, and even after all of their efforts, all of the medicine and surgical procedures, they thought, *He's not going to make it.*

Somewhere deep inside, I was thinking, *We're going to fight this thing.* The war went on, with my subconscious triggering all sorts of systems that allowed my body to fight.

The doctors could give me reasons that had contributed to why I made it. But they couldn't explain what happened. In the end, it comes down to this: there's a will to live in all of us that's so strong that even when the lights are out, it's still going to keep fighting. That's what pulled me out of it. The human desire to live is so great that it can even beat back what should have been the most devastating of blows.

WHO ARE THE SUPERHEROES?

When I woke up, boy did it hurt. Everything hurt.

Before the accident, my best friend and I used to play tennis together. He often joked that whenever I got hurt, no matter how small the injury—a scraped knee—I acted as though it was the end of the world.

"You're my best friend and I love you," he'd say, "but you have the lowest pain tolerance of anyone I know."

Later, he would visit me when I was recovering from each of the countless painful surgeries I had to undergo. He would come in and find me covered in bandages, strapped to the bed, my movement completely restrained because it was the only way to heal.

One day, he looked at me and said, "I can't even imagine what you went through. You've probably been through more physical suffering than anybody on this planet. You were the guy with the lowest pain tolerance, and now, you've probably got one of the highest. Of all the people I might have predicted would not have been able to handle this, you turn into Iron Man."

He said this to me in a joking way, but I took it as a compliment. Because I also knew he meant it.

Still, I'm not special. I'm not Iron Man—or, rather, we all are. You may see yourself as weak, but if you're ever in a situation where you have to fight and endure pain to survive, you will rise to the occasion. You'll find a strength you didn't even know was there.

My friend isn't a tough guy; he's an easygoing comedian. He hasn't had to go through anything like my experience. He said he can't imagine what it's like, and he's right. But it doesn't matter, because if he did actually go through it, I can guarantee you he would fight. And so would you.

This willpower is something that's in all of us. There are plenty of real stories beyond mine to back this up. We don't need comic books to show us how we're all superheroes underneath.

OUR WILL TO FIGHT

There is, of course, a time when it's natural to give up the fight. My parents, who are in their mid-nineties, are finding it harder to do things and aren't enjoying life as much. They've had a long marriage and accomplished many things over the years. So, while they're still fighting to live each day, their survival instinct isn't quite as fierce. They've fought. They've won. They made it all the way.

But when you're young, like I was when I was in the accident, you have so much life ahead of you. Your brain doesn't want you to miss out.

You might be reading all of this and disagreeing. Maybe you truly don't think you have the energy, strength, or mental fortitude to fight for your life. Maybe you don't think it's worth it.

But just know that it's important to remember you're not alone in any battle. You may think you are, but there are plenty of people out there who are pulling for you—some who you know, and some who you've never met.

You also have to understand you're far stronger than you think you are. No matter how hard the battle seems, you have mental and physical strength that's far greater than you can imagine, and far greater than you've ever seen yourself exhibit.

I've had everything thrown at me, including the kitchen sink, and I came out of it. But I'm not a unique person. I had the right amount of luck, and then I took care of the rest. If you're reading this—if you're able to read this— you've probably already got some of that luck, even if you don't think you do (remember, I realized I was lucky when I was covered head to toe in bandages!). Whatever your hardship is, you have the same strength and resilience built into you that I do. We have the exact same wiring. You're just as "special" as I am. So hang in there. I'm one of the people pulling for you.

THE STRENGTH OF HOPE

The body and the brain don't just use strength to help us survive. Our minds also give us hope.

Hope may be the last thing you have. Maybe you've lost everything. Your money may be gone, and people who were important to you may have abandoned you. But nobody can take hope from you. That belongs to you alone—and you don't even need that much. As long as you have even a small amount, it will keep you fighting. Hope means we know there's a chance. And if there's a chance, it's worth fighting for.

No matter how beat up or down and out you are, there's always hope that the next hour, or the next day, or the next week is going to be better. And it can be.

Hang on to that hope. It can be astonishingly strong, if you let it.

That's what I learned as my recovery continued. It appeared I could look forward to sticking around on this earth for a while longer yet. But getting to a full and meaningful life would not be easy, and hope would be necessary to get me through.

Chapter Five

WHEN YOU HEAR THERE'S LITTLE CHANCE

I was facing long odds before I even knew it.

When I was wheeled into the burn unit, unconscious, I was in the best hospital I could hope to be in. I had some of the best burn experts in the world, and even they couldn't guarantee I would make it. When you came right down to it, my problem was purely mathematical.

LONG ODDS

Eighty percent of my body was burned. A third of that was first-degree burns, another third was second-degree burns, and third-degree burns made up the final third.

The reason that my problem was mathematical was because third-degree burns require skin grafts, but to make a skin graft, the skin has to come from your own body. The surgeons could only take skin that hadn't been burned, which means they only had 20 percent or less of my skin to work with.

That's not much.

Luckily, they had perfected a technique where a small patch of skin could be stretched out. To me, it looked like a giant crossword puzzle made up of horizontal and vertical lines of skin. When this stretched grid of skin was stitched on top of a third-degree burn, skin would eventually grow in and fill the holes.

It's a good thing they had mastered this technique. If they hadn't, there is no way the 20 percent of unburnt skin on my body could have covered the sheer amount of third-degree burns on my body.

But it still wasn't a perfect solution. Removing a portion of skin means that you leave behind a wound that's the equivalent of a second-degree burn, which then also has to be treated. It was like a Rubik's Cube: once one problem was solved, another one was created, but it was the only way out.

Having that 20 percent of skin was one more reminder of how lucky I was. But the long odds didn't stop there.

MORE BAD MATH

All of that progress could only go so far. My burns essentially left me covered in open wounds. Like all burn victims, my immune system had all but stopped functioning because all of my body's energy was concentrated on simply staying alive. The risk of infection, therefore, was insanely high. Four or five times as many people die from infections that occur after their burn injury than from the burn itself.

I was surprised when the doctors told me this. I had thought that once I had gotten over the damage from the burns themselves, I would have a good chance of survival. Now, even though I had survived the injuries, there was a huge chance of me dying from an infection.

The hospital was, understandably, paranoid about any kind of infection risk, which is why I couldn't have many visitors and, when I did, they had to be totally cleaned and gowned up.

Despite all the risks and hardships, I made it through, even though it turned out this was less expected than I might have thought.

HELP FROM HISTORY

Some more math came into play in my case: if my accident had happened twenty, or even ten years earlier, I would have spent ten months longer in the burn unit—assuming I survived.

Things had changed so dramatically thanks to another group of people I'm grateful to.

During the Vietnam War, soldiers with my types of burns were dying left and right. This spurred enormous advances in burn victim care management. I feel such gratitude toward those men and women whom I don't even know. Through their suffering and, in many cases, deaths, they spurred the medical community to come up with better ways of helping people like me. God bless all our veterans.

I feel guilty that people had to suffer so I could make it, but unfortunately, this seems to be a common process with any disease or injury. One of the doctors who treated me wrote a research paper on my case, with photographs I gave him permission to take and include in his study. I hope what the doctors have learned from treating *me* has helped people who have been injured in the years since I was hospitalized.

SEVEN PERCENT TO TEN PERCENT

The first time the doctors had to share my near impossible odds for recovery, I wasn't there to hear it. It was when they told my parents there was zero chance I was going to live.

After that, I wasn't necessarily expected to die, but I was still vulnerable to infection, and knew I could still die. The odds still weren't exactly great.

Then, finally, about two months after the doctors had told my parents to expect me to die, Dr. Hunt and Dr. Purdue came into my room. Because they were so busy, it was rare for both of them to be there at the same time.

Okay, I thought suspiciously, *what's this?*

They told me I was going to live, which was great news. But, of course, they had some more bad math for me. "Your arms and sides were badly burned. The odds of you being able to have full range of motion, or even being able to lift your arms more than seven or eight inches from your sides, is very low, at best."

Wait a minute, I thought. *I survived. I'm going to live now. But you're telling me I'm not going to be able to do simple things for the rest of my life?*

"You said the odds aren't good," I pressed. "Give me some numbers."

"As a matter of fact," they said, "the odds are terrible. We could do two surgeries, one for each arm. We would have to do some skin grafting on your left and right sides and arms. Even if we did these two major surgeries, the odds are extremely low that you'll be able to get your full range of motion back."

"Okay," replied, "If you do these surgeries, what kind of chances do I have to regain the full use of my arms? Put a number on it," I told them again. "As a percentage, what are the odds?"

They looked at each other as if they didn't know what to say. Finally, one of them said, "Seven to ten percent."

Even if I underwent two major procedures, with massive investments of money, time, and all of the energy that had to be put into recovery, those were my chances. The doctors were right; the odds weren't good. But they were the only odds I had at being able to live a normal life again.

I looked directly at them and prepared to speak. It was my turn to give them my own calculations.

Chapter Six

———

DECLARE IT'S
UNACCEPTABLE

I've always thought that when someone lays out bad odds for you, it's a challenge. Instead of hearing the doctors' estimates as certain defeat and resigning myself to being disabled for the rest of my life, what I heard was a challenge.

I listened to the numbers they gave me—a 7 to 10 percent chance to have a normal life with full use of my arms.

"That is unacceptable," I told them. And then I gave them some of my own numbers.

"Look," I said, "as long as you're telling me it's not zero, I'm hearing 100 percent."

I knew I'd make it. What I didn't expect was their response.

FINDING THE INNER FIRE

When I told them I was willing to do whatever it took to be able to have a normal life, they both smiled at me. I didn't, at first, know what this meant.

"Why are you two laughing?" I asked. I thought they couldn't believe how stubborn I was being.

It turned out their smiles meant something completely different. They explained, "We needed to see if there's a fire inside you. Most people would view the odds you have and see it as us predicting their defeat, but you take it as a challenge."

They told me the surgeries were very expensive and very long. After that, if it was even possible, regaining the full use of my arms would take at least a year of both physical therapy sessions at the hospital and working on my own.

"We had to make sure you had the right reaction," they said. "We wouldn't invest all the time and money if we thought you weren't going to put in the effort."

Let's stop and think about that for a minute, because it's precisely why finding that fight—that fire they were looking for—is necessary. Sure, I got lucky in lots of ways, but I was also fighting, and without that fight, without my willingness to do the hard work, the doctors wouldn't have been willing to fight alongside me. The fight was necessary.

"I will come back here in a year," I promised them, "and we'll go down to the parking lot, and I'll dunk a basketball for you."

They smiled again, and this time I smiled with them. "We believe you," they told me.

I nodded. "I guarantee you, I will come through."

THE NECESSARY CHOICE

When you face a tragedy, you have two choices. You can either curl up into a ball and be defeated, or declare "This is unacceptable" and fight.

I chose to do the latter. But as I've said, I'm not a super-hero, and I'm not unique. We all have this in us—you just have to summon it. But I know that sometimes it's not easy, or doesn't even seem possible.

During the year I was in physical therapy, I became friends with a guy who came for sessions at the same time as I did. He had some low moments, and I'd tell him we were in this together, and we're going to fight together.

Sometimes he would get teary-eyed during the workouts, and it wasn't just because they were hard. If you looked at my face, you'd probably have no idea that I had been burnt so badly. I had only gotten second-degree burns there, and they had healed nicely. This guy, unfortunately, had more noticeable burn scars on his face.

He told me that everywhere he went, people stared at him. "I can understand what that's like," I told him. "I have scars all over the place and so do you, and yes, you have a few on your face. But I really don't think you look bad at all."

I was telling the truth. I had seen burn patients who had ended up with some really unfortunate facial scarring that would change their lives. His scars, at least, were fairly minor. Still, he didn't look like he once had, and it really bothered him. I tried to remind him he would also look even better as time went on and he healed a bit more. Still, though, the people kept staring, and he became overwhelmed.

I could easily understand why. Dealing with something like that is hard enough on its own, but we were at a point where we still needed physical therapy to move normally.

We both went through hours of stretching exercises and light weight lifting, among other things (since no two burn injuries are the same, PT programs vary from patient to patient). One day he told me, "I can't take the pain anymore. What's the point? I'm not going to make it anyway."

Even though it's hard, even though you're discouraged and at a low point in your life, if you start taking that attitude, that's exactly what's going to happen. Essentially, it's a self-fulfilling prophecy.

He quit in the middle of his recovery. The nurses tried to call him, but he had disappeared. They knew if he didn't continue his sessions, he would end up disabled for the rest of his life. I wish he could have seen the bigger picture. I wish he had learned, as I had, how lucky he was. I wish he'd understood there were so many burn patients who didn't have the options he had to improve his range of motion.

He never came back to physical therapy, and I don't know if he continued on his own. It made me incredibly sad.

CHOOSE TO FIGHT FOR A CHANCE TO WIN

I'm not saying this guy was weak or a lesser person than anyone else. It's easy to understand what he was going through and why he made his choice. But I wish he had thought about things differently. Yes, there is a struggle, but what if the outcome of not fighting is unacceptable? If he wanted to regain movement and live a normal life, he couldn't quit. But if he was willing to fight, it was going to be hard.

It's as if you said to someone, do you want to stay home, or do you want to be sent over into the middle of a war? If you stay home, the enemy will probably win, and if you fight, it's not going to be easy. The outcome, though, makes fighting the only good option for the best future result. When you think about it like that, fighting is really the only option.

A lot of people choose not to go to war. They'd rather stay home. But that's how you lose. Giving up seems like a great idea in the short term. In the long term, it's not. Fight the daily battle and play "the long game." Victory will eventually be achieved.

This man was young, probably only in his twenties. The fight seemed so long to him—it would have taken years. But if he lives to his seventies or eighties, suddenly that doesn't seem like much. Fight now, and in a few years you'll be fine, or quit and live with the negative consequences for the rest of your life. If you make the latter choice, you'll probably look back and wish you'd put up the fight.

THERE'S NO OVERNIGHT SUCCESS

It's important to have a positive mental attitude. But I think another key to overcoming challenges in life is understanding that even though you may overcome them in the end, there's also the hard side. Nothing worthwhile happens without effort or all at once.

We often use the phrase "overnight success." In reality, the people we consider overnight successes were probably working to achieve their goal for years. Once they make it, everyone overlooks those years of struggle. This only makes it harder when the rest of us face a challenge or have something we want to accomplish. We have a warped view of what success really looks like.

The truth is, there is a lot of work involved in any kind of success. There is no such thing as an overnight success. To be frank, I'm not sure any achievement worth talking about has ever come without hard work in the face of adversity.

MORE FIGHT FROM MY MOM

Saying "this is unacceptable" and deciding to fight may not manifest itself the same way for everyone.

After the doctors told my parents I only had a few days at most to live and to look for a priest if they wanted me to be given last rites, my mother surprised everyone in the room with a question: "Well," she said, "let's assume he makes it. Can he still have children?"

The doctors stared at each other. They didn't want to say, "That's a ridiculous question, because it's not going to happen." Instead, they told her, "We'll go along with your thinking here. If for some miraculous reason he makes it, yes, he could have children."

I'm pretty sure when the doctors were alone later, they probably looked at each other and said, "Can you believe we got asked that question? We told her that her son is going to die, and she's thinking about him having kids!"

They wouldn't be the only ones thinking that was a strange question in those circumstances. After my recovery, I laughed when I heard this story. You might think she'd ask if there were other doctors they could bring in, or something else that could be done to save me. Instead, her son was on the verge of death and she was thinking of a grandkid.

Crazy as it sounds, though, there is a lot more to my mother's question than it seems. It certainly wasn't, at that moment, her sense of humor. And it wasn't denial, either. After all, she and my dad were realistic enough to go get a priest. They understood the gravity of what was happening, and they knew the doctors' prognosis was probably right. But in spite of all that, some part of my mom couldn't help thinking, *There is a shot that he's going to pull out of this. And if he does...*

My mother has lived to her mid-nineties and is currently battling bladder cancer. She's a fighter, and her question, I think, was her way of fighting what had happened to me. She saw the odds weren't good, but she jumped ahead to me making it. Asking if I could still have children was her way of saying, "My son dying is unacceptable."

Incidentally, it turned out her question was a good one. I made it, and there is a kid to prove it. My seventeen-year-old son, Jeffrey Thomas (or "JT") is applying to college now.

REMEMBER WHAT YOU'RE FIGHTING FOR

I hope I'm not making it seem like this was easy, or that I kept that sense of humor every excruciating moment of the day. After the two surgeries, my recovery was a herculean effort. I would wake up feeling exhausted and in pain, knowing that I had to do exactly what I'd done the day before. There were plenty of days when I didn't want to get up, when I thought, *I don't want to be me.*

But then I'd remember the alternative. Did I want to

be disabled for the rest of my life? Was it worth living a more limited life—and carrying the regret that would come with it—to save myself some pain in the short term? That option was so unacceptable to me that it always got me back into the fight, even if I wasn't always happy about it. I ingrained the following phrase into my thought process: "pain equals progress." There simply was no easy way out, so I had to embrace the pain (something I know Navy SEALs teach new recruits). I also adopted the motto "Nothing stops the recovery." I couldn't afford a gym membership, so all my exercises were done in city parks. Even in terrible weather, I was always out there fighting. Navy SEALs are heroes—I'm not. But because I had over four years of self-directed recovery experience, I did adopt a great deal of their mental toughness techniques without even realizing it. "Get comfortable being uncomfortable," for example, certainly rang true. I also discovered I liked running my own show and calling my own shots. Life was telling me to become an entrepreneur. Writing this book, in fact, is the first step toward becoming my own boss.

Recovering from a bad burn injury is very different than recovering from a broken leg, sprained ankle, or a torn ACL. With a broken leg, doctors will tell you to stay off your leg and rest. They want you to give your body the chance to heal. A severe burn, on the other hand, is just the opposite. The minute I became an outpatient, the war was on. Skin grafts, and all of the areas that were badly burned, began to contract very rapidly as I was healing. This presented a huge problem. I was fighting to regain the full use of my arms by stretching my grafts and burned skin every day, but my body was trying to heal, which meant I was also fighting against contracting skin. I was essentially swimming against the current. If I gained a few centimeters of additional movement during the day, I would then lose a centimeter during the night as I slept. It was literally two steps forward and one step back. This meant the recovery would take much longer than I first expected. It was a war, because my adversary never took a break—so neither could I. Taking even one day off would mean I was going to start heading in reverse. War is 24/7, and I attacked my adversary every day so I could ensure complete victory.

I did, however, try to make the recovery as fun as possible. Once I was out of the hospital, I listened to music when I exercised (does anyone remember the Sony Walkman?) and brought Sparky with me everywhere. I was responsible for virtually all of my own recovery. No one was there coaching me. It was just Sparky and me. We would walk to the park, and I would do chin-ups and other exercises with her by my side.

Right before I was discharged from the hospital after my initial two-month stay, I asked my burn doctors how

I should design my recovery activities. I assumed they would give me a book, a research paper, or at least a long pep talk. They looked at each other, then back at me, and said, "We actually have no ideas for you."

"What?" I said in disbelief. They explained that in all their years as surgeons, no one burned as badly as me had ever survived. Therefore, they had no clue how I was supposed to proceed. I literally had to design my own two-year recovery program by myself. And I did just that.

A typical day included a five-mile hike, then a trip to the park where I'd do one hundred chin-ups and pull-ups with five-pound weights attached to my ankles. It would take hours to make it to one hundred, but I wouldn't allow myself to go home until I hit my number. My skin would tear regularly, leaving my T-shirts bloody by the time I finally left.

In the end, I was right to fight. The operations and all the hard work following my release from the burn unit have given me twenty-five years of the full use of my arms, so far.

COMING BACK TO HOPE

Declaring that something is unacceptable and deciding to fight, is a show of hope. Nothing motivates me more than when someone tells me something is impossible. If you tell me that most people wouldn't be able to do something, I'll think, *I'm not most people.* When someone says, "You can't," I think, *I'm going to prove you wrong.* The key phrase is "prove them wrong." Nothing is more motivating.

The doctors laid out a bad scenario for me, but it had a bit of hope in it. I clawed onto that and never let go.

If there is a chance and some hope, even a very small amount of it, you have to put it into your head that what you want is going to happen. Then, give it all you've got. There's a good chance you'll make it, but if you don't, at least you tried.

There's nothing worse than not trying. It means you never tried to achieve any other outcome or make a positive outcome a reality. Win or go down swinging.

MY DAY AS A GHOST

I suppose the closest I came to being dead—aside from when I was in the ambulance, of course—was the day at church when I was a ghost.

Let me explain.

About a year after I got out of the hospital, I ran into the ER doctor who had been there the day I was brought in.

I was heading into church, wearing a coat and tie, and someone introduced us. Then he realized who I was.

He looked stunned. "I can't believe you're standing here," he said.

I was still pretty beat up and wearing a burn compression suit under my clothes, but he couldn't imagine I had even gotten that far. As far as he had assumed, I had to be dead.

That morning was one of his first in the ER. He had recently completed his internship and residency. He was hoping this would be a relatively quiet couple of hours.

"You really ruined my morning," he joked. "I thought it was going to be an easy day and then they wheeled you in. I'm trained to do a lot of things, but nothing like the care you needed. I had to call the two lead burn doctors."

What he said made me realize how bad it must have looked. He thought I was going to be in the ground in less than a week. But there I was, standing and talking to him. He said it was like seeing a ghost. He would never have believed we'd be having this conversation. I enjoyed that moment.

Now and then, hope pays off, even in ways you don't expect.

Chapter Seven

—

WHEN YOU FACE A LONG RECOVERY

During the second month I was in the hospital, I had to have three more surgeries. When the nurse told me that, I told her I was nervous. I had never had surgery before in my life, not even for something fairly common like appendicitis or tonsillitis.

What I didn't recall was that I'd already had two major surgeries during my medically induced coma, and she reminded me of that. It was surprising news to me, to say the least. Over the next two years, I would have fifteen more surgeries. Some were easier than others, but none of those recoveries are particularly happy memories.

Some were downright awful.

UNBEARABLE PAIN AND INCREDIBLE RELIEF

The first order of business was to cover all of my third-degree burns with skin grafts. This was the main goal of the first four operations. It couldn't be done all at once, because of how long each surgery takes and the number of wounds the surgery would create as my healthy skin was used to make all the skin grafts.

The third surgery went as expected, but the fourth was another story.

The night before a surgery, the doctor would come to talk to me about what was going to happen and what to expect. This time, one of the burn doctors told me, "This one is going to be pretty easy."

"Really?" I asked. "What does easy mean?"

"Well," Dr. Hunt replied, "we don't have as much to do this time, and so you probably won't be under as long." He explained where they were going to graft and where I would see bandages: "It's not a total guarantee, but it's pretty close to being accurate," he said.

I repeat, these guys are some of the best in the world. But sometimes, even the best can't know everything. During the surgery, the doctors looked at my body and decided they had to do double or triple what they had planned to do.

As I was coming out of the anesthesia hours later, I was shocked by how many bandages I had. *This wasn't even close to what they told me to expect*, I thought. Then things got crazy.

I started to feel more and more pain, until it began to hit me at a level I had never felt before in my life. The pain was indescribable. My surgeons told me there is nothing more painful that a bad burn injury. If you've ever been to a hospital, you've probably had someone ask you, "On a scale of one to ten, how would you describe your pain?" Mine wasn't even on that chart. It wasn't ten, it was *one hundred* and ten, and going higher by the second.

During everything I went through, I had until this time only cried once, when I'd heard that young Eric had died. Now the pain was so strong, so unbearable, that I started crying again.

Should I have been in this much pain? By now, a fair number of people had gathered in my room. They must have been panicking and wondering what had gone wrong.

A nurse came in with the biggest hypodermic needle I have ever seen. It was full of morphine. "This is the biggest dose we can give you," she explained, careful not to add the other part...*without killing you.*

She pinched my hip and injected the morphine. Within sixty seconds, an incredible, warm, fuzzy feeling flew up from my toes, all the way to my head. Sixty seconds before, I had been in more pain than I had ever felt in my life. With that injection, I don't think I'd ever felt that good.

I started to get a bit loopy. The nurses stared in surprise: sixty seconds earlier, they had seen me in incredible suffering; now I was cracking jokes.

"This morphine is really good," I remember saying.

Once the pain was managed, I was fine, and I'm glad I got the worst surgery out of the way when I did. Not all of the others to come would be easy, but at least I was prepared. What I wasn't fully prepared for was the fact that once I left the hospital, I'd realize my recovery had only just begun.

LEAVING THE HOSPITAL

Walking out of the hospital wasn't easy—in fact, it wasn't even possible for a long time, given that I had to learn to walk again.

Once a day, two nurses would come to my room, and I'd put one arm around each. (I'll admit it helped that they happened to be very nice and quite cute.) They'd walk me down the hall and back to my room. My "graduation" was walking down three stairs and back up, with their help. It was a huge deal.

The day I left the hospital, I was so excited to go home, but getting from the wheelchair to the car was a monumental effort. I was wheeled to the hospital door by one of my nurses, then there was a short walk to where my first wife had parked our car. It was only about thirty yards, but after I had walked about five or six yards, I was holding on to the wall, too weak to continue. I finally made it, but it took what seemed like an hour.

When I got home, I put on my pajamas and just collapsed onto the couch. Sparky jumped up and curled up with me. That's how I spent my first evening back home: just lying on the couch with my dog, watching TV with my wife.

It was great to be home. If you've ever been in the hospital, you'll know what I mean. Once you get out, you feel a sense that normalcy is returning. You think, *Okay, if I'm home, things have to be getting better.*

However, I was far from done with the hospital. I'd have to return for daily physical therapy, Monday through Friday, for the next year. I would also have to continue with the one-hour debriding sessions for the first month or so. My first appointment was the day after my return home.

Not long after I'd started this new routine, I found out there was something about my life that the doctors thought was pretty funny, and I had to agree: I was a burn victim with a dog named Sparky. Many fire departments have a mascot dog named Sparky.

WORKING TOWARD NORMAL

Even though I was out of the hospital, I wasn't just returning for physical therapy. There were still many surgeries I had to undergo. My reconstructive surgeon, Dr. Rohrich, and I would joke about how many surgeries I'd had. "How many is it again?" I'd ask him with a laugh.

"A lot," he'd answer. We had both lost count.

After each surgery, I'd have to stay in the hospital for a week of recovery, immobile the entire time so my body could heal and the skin grafts would stay in place. Luckily, as I've said, I had friends who would come and visit. Still, it wasn't easy. After that, I would have a month or two surgery-free and, when they felt I'd been given enough time to heal, I'd have to come back in for another surgery.

When I wasn't being operated on or in recovery, I continued my daily physical therapy sessions. These were held in a huge room in the hospital, where I was surrounded by a number of other recovering burn patients. The room was full of machines and exercise tables. When a burn victim like me arrived, the staff would wrap our skin grafts with warm wax, towels, and lubricants to keep the grafts moisturized. It helped dull the pain and make stretching easier.

As I progressed, I would use different machines. My legs weren't a problem; for me, it was getting back the use of my arms. The therapists' primary focus was helping me stretch out my left and right arms and sides, and helping me regain muscle mass by lifting weights—very light ones at first, but I progressed over time. After all, the doctors had told me I'd never raise my arms over my head again. In turn, I'd told them I'd be dunking a basketball one day. I had to keep that challenge in mind.

I had lost an incredible amount of muscle mass. I weighed 185 pounds before the injury. When I started outpatient physical therapy, I weighed just 140 pounds. Compared to the guy I used to see in the mirror, I felt like a skeleton. I wanted to get that muscle back.

The therapy worked well, and by year two of my recovery, it was completely self-directed exercises outside the hospital. Now, it was just me, Sparky, and the chinning bar in the park.

ON MY OWN WITH SPARKY

Now I was really on my own. No physical therapists pushing me, no doctors guiding me. Just Sparky and my first wife.

There was a really nice park near my house, with lots of grass and a lake. It was close to Love Field airport, so Southwest Airlines jets would fly over me as they came into Dallas. That was fun to watch. The park was free, of course, and Sparky loved being outside, so it was the perfect place to go for my workouts.

At the park, I'd tie Sparky to a tree near me, and she'd just watch while I worked toward my hundred chin-ups and pull-ups.

It was hard, but I was committed. I worked out so hard that my arms were extremely tired and heavy by the time I left. When I would get home and shower, it was almost impossible for me to lift them to shampoo my hair. I would laugh at myself sometimes, because I'd do all that work, but it was the shampooing that was painful and difficult. Still, I took it as a good sign—if it's hard to shampoo your hair, that means you put in the hard work.

I have a lot of good memories from my time in the park. I love the outdoors, and of course, anything was better than being in a hospital. I was making progress. After two years of recovery, not only could I use my arms the way I had been able to before, I had increased my muscle mass to the point that I sailed past my previous weight of 180 pounds and was now 215. I knew it was muscle, because I was wearing the same size pants I'd worn before. I might have been scarred, but in some ways, I'd never looked better.

On a more serious note, my battle was also much like a war. The battlefield changed every day—war is not static. In a two-year period, I had sixteen or seventeen major surgeries (at some point, even my doctors lost count) and each surgery changed the way I had to fight the enemy. I was forced to quickly adapt on the fly. New surgeries and healing skin and skin grafts required new strategies. My workouts had to be adjusted to the new reality of each passing day.

I had to become skilled at rapidly adjusting to change, and I did. This made my situation more challenging, but also more interesting. They say that sometimes when you recover from tragedy, you come out the other side stronger. With enough work, I made that true in more ways than one.

Chapter Eight

SIMPLIFY THE PROCESS

My recovery was an experiment. Eighty percent of my body had been covered in burns. The doctors and staff had never seen anyone in my situation survive. In short, they didn't know what my recovery would be like. They knew I had a long road ahead, but no one could say just how long it would be. We just knew it would be long and painful, and the light at the end of the tunnel was far off and very dim.

I was facing the unknown, which is something many people can identify with. No matter what you're going through, that's often how it feels. Even if it is something others have gone through, it's new territory for you, and it can be scary. It's overwhelming. That's why you have to simplify the process of recovery.

HOUR BY HOUR

I was certainly overwhelmed when the doctors told me they couldn't give me an actual timeframe for my recovery. At first, like many people, I looked at my problem the wrong way, and all I saw was this long, unknown future, a quest so long and painful, with so many things that could go wrong. It was simply too much to take in. I had the feeling that many people have when faced with such a situation. There was a voice whispering to me, "Why even try?" It would be easier to accept life how it was than to do the enormous amount of work necessary to have just a chance at something better.

If I had listened to that voice, it would have gotten the best of me. Too many surgeries, too much time, too much effort to make, too many things that could go wrong. It could have made me give up.

Through trial and error, I realized it was best to break the recovery down into manageable parts—not month to month or week to week, but day by day. Even hour by hour.

I would think about what I was going to do or accomplish today, not tomorrow. I wouldn't think about the surgery scheduled two weeks from now; I'd worry about it when it got here. Focusing on the day and the hour was the only way to stay in the game without blowing a gasket.

Later, when I'd go to the park, I would only ask myself, "What am I going to do in the next couple of hours?" I would forget about tomorrow or even tonight. I lived in the present and didn't worry about what was to come.

It was vital to work at staying focused in the moment. My mind wandered, and I found myself thinking, *Oh my God, how am I going to keep doing this for the next 365 days?* But I learned to notice those thoughts, and I'd stop myself. *No*, I'd think, *what am I going to do today?* I would give myself a short-term goal for that day, that hour, or that moment, then work like crazy to accomplish it.

That's how I got through my recovery, by breaking it down into manageable segments. When you think of things that way, it seems much easier to do what you have to. When you're simply dealing with the day or even the hours ahead, you can say, "Well, I can do that."

I later learned what I was doing is called "compartmentalization." It was a critical strategy to make my recovery a success, but it's also used by entrepreneurs, soldiers, and others to help navigate through especially stressful situations. I stumbled upon this mind-strengthening strategy through sheer necessity. You'd be amazed at the productive brainstorming you do when your back is against the wall.

THE NEED FOR PATIENCE

Recognizing the need for patience was crucial to my recovery, especially when it came to regaining the full use of my arms. Every day I would work hard, pushing myself and making progress. Then, at night, my scars and skin grafts would contract, which is how they heal. The next day, I would have to regain some of the ground I'd already gained the day before, and then try to advance further. It was, essentially, two steps forward and one step back. You might pick up a few centimeters of extra movement during the day, but the rapid skin and scar contraction would usually negate about half of that progress each night.

The strides I made on any given day were imperceptible. Only after a month or so would I be able to notice I could lift my arms a little bit higher than before. I had long-term goals, and I had to learn to be patient and wait to until a large enough amount of time had passed to make my progress perceptible. As counterintuitive as it may sound, staying focused on the present moment and those smaller, manageable tasks was the best way to get through those long, difficult stretches.

I came to appreciate even the smallest chunks of progress. I knew that those centimeters I gained would add up to inches, and those inches would add up to even more.

At the end of two, long years, I was able to touch my hands over the top of my head like a man about to dunk a basketball.

SMALL VICTORIES, SMALL REWARDS

Human beings thrive on manageable tasks and on rewards. So, in addition to giving myself daily goals that kept me grounded in the moment, I also gave myself rewards for accomplishing those smaller goals. These became crucial for me, especially since there were times when I couldn't see any progress toward the long-term goal. But when I rewarded myself, I was seeing a result. There was something empowering in that—being able to give myself these rewards when I saw signs of progress.

This goes back to dealing with the present moment, instead of obsessing over what was coming. I would think, *What am I doing today?* and then, *What's my reward?*

I broke the long-term goal of regaining the use of my arms into little victories to celebrate along the way. I would think, *Okay, today I hit a pretty big target, so now I'll go see that new movie everyone's talking about.*

Give yourself little rewards along the way. It will keep you motivated.

RECOVERY IS NOT A CHOICE

Another strategy I had during this time was to make my recovery nonnegotiable. My mindset was "relentless attack."

Every day, I would wake up thinking, *Recovery is what I do. It's my job.*

Even when I was out of the hospital and on my own, I kept this attitude. In fact, once I was on my own, it became that much more important to have this mindset. Nothing stopped the recovery, not even the weather. It could be raining outside, or 110 degrees, or snowing. I would go out in pouring rain, scorching heat, freezing temperatures. There were no excuses. The weather only meant I'd have to put on a raincoat or jacket. If it was hot, tough! I'd just have to find a place to work out in the shade.

Once, I headed out with Sparky into an absolute monsoon of a rainstorm. Labradors love water, but even she was giving me a look. If she could have talked, she would have said, "I love you and I love the outdoors, but come on, this is ridiculous."

But day in, day out, we went outside—there was no such thing as a day off with this job.

I don't mean to steal from Nike, but, basically, you do

have to have a "just do it" mentality. Don't think about it, don't *over*think it. You know what you need to do, so just go out and do it. No excuses; no "this is going to hurt." I shut that part of my brain off and became like a machine. I had a job to do, and I did it. You literally become "addicted to the grind," so tough days were the norm. Pain isn't a bad thing—pain equals progress.

CROSS TODAY'S BRIDGE

My progress was slow, but even if I had gained a small amount of motion after a certain amount of time, it was still a victory. I could take pride in that as I looked back on my day.

When it came to seeing those small victories, instead of only focusing on my larger goal, there was a phrase I started to use: "Cross today's bridge."

Each day, I was crossing a bridge and trying to make it to the other side. When I did, even if the victory was small, it was still a victory. In the end, all of those small victories added up to me winning the war.

After two years, I could use my arms. I had extra muscle mass. I was fit and healthy and looked great. I was proud of myself for hanging in there and gaining ground, small victory by small victory.

I didn't just have to work on myself physically. I also had to work through some intense emotions. One day I may have been extremely productive, but the next morning I would wake up "fighting mad," as I came to call it. I was mad at the world, and I was, well, just plain *angry*. Anger is a very powerful force, but it can easily lead to destructive behavior. Some people will turn to alcohol or drugs, or even resort to crime and violence. None of these things get you anywhere positive. I came to accept the fact I'd have tough, angry days, and chose to use anger to my advantage. I call it "focused rage." I channeled my anger and aggression into productive activities like my workout. I ended up having some of my best days when I felt angry. The chin-ups and pull-ups were easier, and I usually did more than I had planned. By the end of the day I was exhausted, and I couldn't even remember what I had been so mad about. I'd head home in a great mood with a very productive day behind me.

Chapter Nine

WHEN YOU THINK YOU'RE LEFT WITH NOTHING

Two years after the accident, all of those small victories added up. I had regained nearly 100 percent range of motion in both of my arms. My left arm, because of how damaged it was, would always be a bit tighter than my right—but hey, I'm right-handed, and besides, I was stronger than I'd ever been before. Looking back, I couldn't believe all I had overcome. I trusted the process, and it worked.

I had beaten something that looked insurmountable, something I could never have seen coming. I was proud of myself and, more than anything, ready to move on and get back to a normal life.

There was just one more surgery I needed to have, but after losing count of my surgeries, it didn't seem like a big deal. I began to look for jobs, letting potential employers know I might have to miss one week of work at some point, which no one seemed particularly worried about.

We had had to sell the house and were currently living in a rental. It wasn't really an issue for me, though, since I had been so wrapped up in my recovery. I was just glad Sparky and everyone else I loved was fine and that life was going to go on. I was confident a good job would come along and I could once again help my wife pay the monthly bills.

Then one day, I came home from a long day of looking for work and found our rental almost completely empty.

LEFT WITH NOTHING...ALMOST

My wife had left and had taken just about everything in the house—including most of the money in our bank accounts—with her. About all that was left was an old couch and an old bed in the place where the king-sized bed we slept in used to be. Sparky was just sitting on the hardwood floor—smiling, as she always did.

About an hour later, my wife came in and handed me a $300 check. "I'm done—I didn't sign up for this," she told me. I guess "for richer or poorer, in sickness and in health" truly meant nothing to her. I had too much to worry about to get upset about the stark reality that she had married me for my income potential. Well, live and learn.

We had two cars. She took the good one and was gone. She didn't tell me where she was going to live—in fact, she told me nothing. I found out later that her parents had flown to town and helped her clean out all of our good furniture and anything of value.

I couldn't believe it, and I couldn't explain it. Later, I would learn she had been unfaithful to me for years. To her credit, about a year later (after the divorce was final), she came clean. I ran into her by accident while I was walking Sparky and asked her about the rumors I had heard, and she admitted that, yes, she'd been having an affair with my dentist while I was in the hospital.

While she was talking, I looked down at Sparky. Dogs never forget anyone they've met—especially someone they've shared a home with. When I ran into my ex-wife and we were discussing the dentist, I noticed that Sparky paid absolutely no attention to her at all. Her tail didn't wag, and she really acted like my former wife was a complete stranger. I think Sparky knew exactly who she was, and that she was someone who could not be trusted. A dog's instinct is never wrong.

She said both she and the dentist felt badly about their behavior, and she even said my dentist would enjoy having me back as a patient. I said nothing, but, as you would guess, I found a new dentist.

In retrospect, it was probably for the best that I didn't know about her adultery during my recovery, but still, even years later, it stung to know that while I was fighting for my life I could be so betrayed. Evil comes into your life in many forms (we all know the "wolf in sheep's clothing" story), but my book is not about betrayal, adultery, infidelity, or abandonment, so we'll move on.

On the day she left, I didn't know what to feel. I had just overcome the biggest obstacle of my life—I had literally spent two years fighting to have this life, and now it was gone. Everything was gone.

Well, no. Not everything.

Once my wife had driven away, I sat down on the hardwood floor, next to Sparky.

I couldn't help it. Maybe it was my mom's sense of humor showing up to save me again, maybe I was in shock, but I looked at Sparky, and I smiled.

"Well," I said to her, "now what?"

RETURNING TO WORK

In addition to Sparky, I also had that whopping $300 check, but it was clear that wasn't going to take me very far. Now I needed a job more than ever.

The bills kept arriving in my mailbox. Rent. Credit card bills. Landlords and banks don't care what's going on with you, your relationship, or your health—they just want their money.

I had been looking for a corporate job that was comparable to what I'd been doing before, but now, I didn't have the security or time for a targeted job search. Suddenly, instead of planning for maybe a month of interviewing for positions and hopefully returning for follow-up interviews, I was thinking, "I need a job today."

This was back in the good old days before the internet, so I grabbed a newspaper and started looking for something that would pay me enough to survive.

I ended up becoming a car salesman. There are many people who are happy at this job and who have had training and know the business. For me, the job was a nightmare. It was six days a week, twelve hours a day of being treated like garbage and making just enough money to pay the bills, pay the rent, and feed my dog.

After nine months, I couldn't take it anymore. Life had already run me into the ground once, and now I was volunteering for further beatings every day in an environment where all that mattered was getting that sale. I saw a lot of people come and go there, and eventually I became one of them. There's nothing wrong with selling cars, but it was definitely not for me. I hadn't fought so hard just so this could be my life. So I left. No more working at cruel Cadillac.

I'd fought my way back to a better life and a stronger version of myself. Now it was time to take the next step. It was time to get started the right way on recovering my work life.

Chapter Ten

———

YOU'RE MET WITH UNCONDITIONAL LOVE AND PURPOSE

My life had been stripped down to a point where I had almost nothing. But luckily, I had some lessons from my first lightning strike to get me through.

For one thing, I was able to remember that I still had hope. For another, I was fortunate enough to have a loyal dog who gave me unconditional love. Sparky kept me from feeling lonely. She was by my side through everything, regardless of what happened.

People in your life may not be able to help you, or they may disappear on you, but a dog will love you and be there for you. Dogs don't care if you look like Ryan Reynolds or if you're covered in bandages. A dog doesn't care whether you're healthy or sick, rich or poor, homeless or living in a mansion. They will not leave your side. They are the perfect example of unconditional love.

Sometimes, I'll see a homeless person with a dog, and although, of course, I wish they were better off, I can't help reflecting that their dog is probably happy just being with them. It's that simple for a dog, and it's something you learn, especially when that unconditional love is all you have left.

When everybody else seemed to disappear (the divorce led to the disappearance of some friends), I had a companion who was with me during every step of my recovery. Now I was in a new crisis, but Sparky didn't care. We were in this together. I knew that if we could make it through the past two years, we'd make it through this. The burn recovery was essentially a great lesson in "crisis management," so handling being blindsided was rapidly becoming my new specialty.

UNCONDITIONAL LOVE FROM UNEXPECTED PLACES

People who've had a special connection with a pet will understand what I'm talking about. But even if you've never had a pet in your life, maybe you've been lucky enough to have a parent, friend, or loved one who's had your back no matter what you've gone through. However, even if you've had none of that kind of support, I can tell you from experience—as I mentioned earlier—you're really never alone. Sometimes unconditional love and support can come from unexpected places.

When my accident happened, I was young and had a lot of friends, but I found out that being around suffering or hardship is too much for some people, no matter how much they want to support you—and so, they disappear. What I also found out is that people you might have considered secondary or tertiary friends, people you might talk to only once every six months or every few years, people who may have only recently found out about what happened to you, will sometimes step forward.

These people, who might even be barely more than acquaintances, will say, "I want to help you any way I can." They may ask what they can do, or even offer something. I had a friend I hadn't talked to in a long time. He'd gotten married, and I hadn't even met his wife. They heard about what happened to me in the fire and, when my wife left, they came to me with an offer.

"We're moving to Houston," they said, "and we own a house in Dallas, not far from you. The house is on the market now, but we can pull it off and let you and Sparky live there as long as it takes for you to recover and find a job and get back on your feet."

I couldn't believe it. They would essentially continue to own and pay for two homes so that I could stay in one of them with my dog for free until I could take care of myself. Because of all the expenses involved, this would cost them thousands of dollars. It was incredibly generous, and, in the end, I couldn't let them do it. Still, I'll never forget what they offered. They would have spent all that money on me because they saw what I was going through and just wanted to help.

Their offer was a reminder of the lessons I had learned in the ambulance and at the hospital—you're never really alone. There are people out there who have your back, even when you least expect it.

UNCONDITIONAL LOVE AND SUPPORT ONLINE

My story about my friends is touching, but, of course, not everyone in a tough situation gets an offer like that. To me, it's not even so much about the offer to live in a house. The lesson here is there are people who genuinely care. These days, it's even easier to find the kind of support I found—people who care.

If you still feel like you're alone, there is one advantage you have that I didn't when all of these challenges happened to me: the internet.

There are a lot of bad things about the internet, of course, but there are great things about it, too. One of those great things is it helps you realize you're not alone.

No matter your calamity, no matter where you're located, there are support groups out there. All you have to do is Google the terms that pertain to your situation and you'll find people to talk to.

Over the years, I've connected with so many people online. For example, I had already recovered from my burns when the internet became popular, but I joined a burn victims' support group, and I use my spare time to help others who are going through what I did. One way I try to help is by following them on Twitter and retweeting their requests for help, hoping they might find their way to other people who are able to lend them a hand.

One of the things I like most about support groups is that nowadays most of them offer different ways to get in touch; it doesn't just have to be via an online forum or social media. If you want to talk to someone, they have a phone number. If you'd be more comfortable writing, they have an email address or sometimes online or text messaging.

Not only is it easy to find a support group, it probably won't take long to make friends with someone who will listen to you and understand because they've been through the same thing. Some group members or volunteers can even help you find local on-site support groups, if you prefer to do that.

If you're not internet savvy, you can contact your hospital or, if you're a burn victim, burn unit and ask them if there is a support group. I'm almost certain they could give you at least a few phone numbers.

LOVE AND SUPPORT AT THE HOSPITAL

During my injury and recovery, another place I found love and support was the hospital itself, which surprised me. Before the accident, I was familiar with a corporate environment, so for a well-paid doctor or nurse to be supportive made sense. But at a big hospital, especially one the size of Parkland, there are thousands of other kinds of people working there who genuinely care about patients as well.

For example, let's take one of my doctors, Dr. Rohrich. When I met him twenty-five years ago, he was working seven days a week. Six of them were spent doing reconstructive surgery for people who had been in all sorts of accidents. The other day, he worked at his private plastic surgery clinic.

One day, I asked him about this and he told me, "Jeff, honestly, I do reconstructive surgery because I care. At my clinic, I do plastic surgery for people who are trying to be more attractive. These are very expensive procedures that aren't covered by insurance, and doctors make a lot of money doing them. The work I do here at Parkland, six days a week, doesn't make me a lot of money, so that's what I have to do on the seventh."

I was stunned. He could have worked five days a week doing plastic surgery for well-to-do people who just want to look better and have had a very lucrative life. But he cared about people like me, and wanted to put in so much time to help us.

Like the hospital workers, he showed me there are people out there who care about you even if they don't know you personally. They care about people who are in need.

In the corporate world I knew before the accident, I always had my eye on the bottom line, how much money I had and what the stock prices were. But here was this other world just a few miles from our offices, where people were putting in every ounce of effort they had, just to help people. Spending time in this environment gave me a different perspective. I realized that there was more to life than the one I'd been living.

COMPASSION AND CONNECTION

My recovery was largely related to my mental state. I've talked about how I had to motivate myself, how I had to refuse to accept what the doctors told me, and push on. But it wasn't something I did completely on my own. (Remember, you're not alone!)

One of the physical therapists I worked with during my first year of outpatient recovery became a friend of mine. Her name is LaDonna. I could tell she loved what she did, and we enjoyed seeing each other. She worked with many patients every day, but she really cared about how each of us was moving and feeling. She'd watch us on the machines, happy we were able to do a little more each day. Setting goals for myself was never a problem, but it was still nice to have someone cheering me on.

She wasn't the only one. Among fellow patients and hospital staff, there was a feeling we were all on the same team. Sometimes another patient might encourage me as I was struggling on a machine. Another day, I'd do the same for someone else. We were all pulling for each other. I know this was important, and not only because of the positive mental energy it created. Sometimes, I would wake up thinking, *Boy, another day of this.* Knowing I would be surrounded by people who wanted me to recover and who were just as happy as I was when I made progress helped me carry on, day after day.

FINDING PURPOSE

Before the accident and the other events that would change my life, I was a corporate guy whose goal was to be a millionaire by the time I was thirty-five. I was no financial wizard, but when I think of all the goals I was setting for myself, I realize they were all about money and acquiring possessions.

After the Blue Sky Lightning struck, I came to realize there were a lot of other people out there, and not all of them had it so good. As I watched other burn patients making progress, getting discharged, and moving on, I was sometimes sad to see them go, especially if it meant I was losing a roommate who had become a friend. But I also felt glad for them. I got joy from their accomplishments, not just my own. My life's focus shifted. I realized none of us are alone. We're all fighting our own battles.

Added to this new perspective was a deep sense of gratitude. So many people have done so many things for me—doctors, nurses, friends, family, and, of course, Sparky. Even the insurance companies that helped me pay my hospital bills were there for me. I may not be able to pay everyone back directly, but I want to give back by helping other people (and animals—more on this later) in need.

After everything I've learned and experienced, I don't see things with a "me" attitude; I see we're all in this together, and I ask myself what I can do for others.

Of course, some people come to the same conclusion as they get older. But when you're young, like I was, you think you're going to live forever. As time passes, you realize you're not going to be here forever. Because of the accident, facing my mortality was just expedited by a few decades. And, in a strange way, I'm incredibly grateful for what happened.

When you realize you're not going to be here indefinitely, you start to wonder what you can do between now and the time you're gone to make a difference. It could be living for your kids, but even more than that, I think it's good to help out beyond your small circle. How can you make this world a better place?

THE SECRET OF HAPPINESS

One way you can do this is by volunteering, which, let me tell you, doesn't have to be drudgery. There are so many charities and organizations that need help that you'll be able to find one you're interested in and enjoy. For example, I love animals, so my son and I work with the Humane Society. We do a lot of work, but we also have a really good time. When we're with the cats and dogs for a few hours, we see how happy they are to have our affection, and it makes us happy, too.

I truly believe when you do things strictly for yourself, the happiness you feel is an empty happiness. When you do things for others, the happiness you get back is light years more rewarding.

You've probably heard people say, "Oh, I'm happy for you." You may not be sure if you believe them. I do. At least I want to, because I know taking joy in others' successes and accomplishments, whether it's your child or someone who's suffering, is a stronger feeling than how you might feel even about your own victories. Seeing someone who was down and out making it back is an incredible source of happiness.

I think that's the real secret of life: taking joy in others' good fortune.

Chapter Eleven

WHEN YOU'RE WITHOUT ANSWERS

My recovery from the fire took me two years. That's a long time to recover, but at first I didn't see it as a long time out of the workforce. Once I was ready to return to work, I learned quickly that technology progresses. The economy continues to go up and down. Between the time I was hospitalized in 1989 to the time I was ready to work again, the real estate market, which I had been working in for years, had gone into a recession—something I, of course, had been completely unaware of.

Things change in other ways, too. People move on. They get married or move away. Time didn't freeze. Instead, it was as if when I was injured I stepped into a time machine.

Suddenly, it was two years later and a whole different ball game.

GETTING BY

I thought that after all I had been through, finding a job would be easy, but it was a lot harder than I thought. Regardless of the academic credentials and work history I had, after being out of the workforce for two years, the world wasn't exactly waiting for me with open arms, ready to hand me another great job.

Two years' absence made me seem a bit like "damaged goods" to potential employers, no matter how sympathetic they were about what I had gone through and how appreciative they were of my qualifications and experience. From a corporate perspective, my long absence meant I just wasn't the same person I'd been.

Between that struggle and the situation I found myself in when my wife left me with $300 and a lot of bills to pay, I took some unexpected jobs to keep a roof over my head. After I left the car dealership, I was surprised to find myself working as a bartender for a while. Actually, the job also involved helping the owners build the bar, so I was a minimum wage construction worker first, *then* a bartender. There were some good things about that work, but ultimately, it wasn't for me, so I moved on.

A friend of mine told me about an opportunity, which ended up being outbound telemarketing. The person who interviewed me assured me it was a great position and that I'd make a lot of money, and, anyway, I needed the work, so I took it.

As I'd feared, outbound telemarketing was even worse than car sales. There was a quota of about seventy calls a day that had to be a certain number of minutes long, and I had to close a certain number of deals. I sat in a small cubicle for the day, and from the time I arrived to the time I left, I was being monitored. I was grateful for many things at that time—including simply being alive— but still, I couldn't wait to get out of work every day and go walk Sparky.

I never felt completely down, though, because I knew I wouldn't be doing these jobs forever. I had faith the right thing would come along. I just had to hang in there. My first recovery had taught me the art of patience and embracing the present moment. *Anyway*, I would think, *this is nothing compared to what I've been through.*

I thought things could never be that bad again. Lightning doesn't strike in the same place twice.

Don't ever make the mistake of saying "It can't possibly get any worse." It can.

SUDDEN PAIN

I remember the day it started like it was yesterday. It was otherwise an insignificant day. I was working at the telemarketing job, and my thighs started to ache. I didn't think much of it at first. Even after my recovery, I had continued to do a lot of walking and working out, so I thought I had just overdone it a bit the day before.

Then the aches in my thighs started spreading, first to my calves and then to other parts of my body. Within a month or two, I was virtually incapacitated. I couldn't work, walk, or even leave the house—not even to do something simple like grocery shopping. Finally, the pain became so excruciating I called my parents about it. They were living out of state, and they flew in to see what was going on.

They took me to several doctors, starting with a regular family doctor. After undergoing some tests, I found out I was suffering from some sort of neuromuscular illness. I had gotten to know many different types of doctors during and after my burn injuries, and in that time I had become something of an expert on burns. Now, I entered a world of medicine that was completely new to me. Luckily, the doctors I came across in this field were also really good at what they did—and good people, as well. They started monitoring my nervous system and running tests, including spinal taps. If you've never had a spinal tap, just know they're not fun, to put it mildly.

The discomfort of having my spine punctured wasn't the worst of it. I was still in a horrendous amount of pain from whatever was wrong with me. In the months after my burn accident, my doctors had told me there's no pain worse than a severe burn injury, especially a catastrophic one like mine. But with this new issue, I was amazed to discover the pain was as bad as a third-degree burn. I had already hit the top of the pain scale, and now I hit it again. We ferried from doctor to doctor. Everyone was convinced that, sooner or later, we'd figure out what was wrong. But until we knew, there was no way to know what to give me for the pain.

ANOTHER UNCERTAIN FUTURE

I believe the doctors did their best to figure out what was wrong with me. In the end, all they could really do, however, was guess. One idea was that I had ALS, commonly called Lou Gehrig's disease. There were other guesses as well—all diseases that were just as grim, if not more so. They thought perhaps it could be multiple sclerosis, but it didn't exactly look like that. They ruled out muscular dystrophy and Guillain-Barré syndrome, an autoimmune disease that attacks the muscular system. They only were certain about one thing: whatever I had would be slow, excruciating, and fatal.

All I could think was, *You've got to be kidding me.* I had just gotten out of a situation where I was supposed to die. I had been given last rites. I had been a few hours away from death, and I had painfully battled my way out of that. I felt I'd earned another shot at life. And now I was hit with another, terminal condition. I'd been in and out of the gates of hell once, and now I was headed back.

There wasn't much hope. But there was still something. I'd already learned you didn't need much hope. When I was badly burned, they told me I had a 7 percent to 10 percent chance of regaining full range of motion, which to me meant I had a 100 percent chance. And now, since they couldn't put a name on what I had, they couldn't be completely sure of anything. That was what I held on to. A disease with no name may not be fatal.

NO ANSWERS AND NO RELIEF

We continued seeing doctors and doing tests, but no answers came. At one point, my father even said we should travel out of state to the Mayo Clinic. We didn't end up doing that. Instead, I ended up just living with it, hoping we'd get answers. We thought we were facing the unknown with the burn injury, since no one like me had ever survived, but at least in the burn unit they knew how to treat burns. Now we didn't even know what was wrong with me. Unlike the burn injury, for which I could have surgeries that would eventually help me get better, I now spent time virtually incapacitated. Even to do something simple like go to the bathroom, I'd have to get down on all fours and crawl to the toilet, and then crawl back into bed.

After recovering from my burn accident and physically improving, looking forward to a normal life and one day having a job I liked, I was suddenly worse off than I'd been in a long time. I couldn't even walk anymore, let alone work out. I diminished from a muscular 215 pounds back to my pre-recovery weight of 140. I continued to experience extreme pain. I had just been reentering the world, and now I was forced out of it again.

I saw more doctors, hoping one might have an answer for me. But each one I visited was at a loss. I was put on some medications to see if they would do anything, but they might as well have been placebos. One doctor who really wanted to help me did something I don't think I had ever seen any other doctor do before. Many people in that profession have full bookshelves in their offices. I always thought these books were there to impress patients with how much they had studied and read. But this doctor actually went to his bookshelves and started pulling down books and thumbing through them, trying to find anything that could lead him to an answer. Unfortunately, he couldn't.

I spent a year of my life bouncing between doctors or

lying in bed in horrible pain while everyone around me tried to figure out what was wrong and how to fix it.

GREEN BUDS IN A CHARRED LANDSCAPE

One day, a specialist decided to do a muscle/nerve biopsy procedure (yes, more surgery). Looking back on that time, I don't know why it took so long for someone to think of that. I can still see the scar where they cut into my right calf.

When they got the results back, the doctor told me something very interesting and very strange. There was good news and bad news. My nerves and muscle tissue, he said, looked like a beautiful forest that had been ravaged by a fire. The trees had fallen down, and everything was dead. "But," he added, "I can see little green buds all over this charred landscape, which means the nerves and muscles are coming back."

He couldn't explain why. He also didn't know why they had been damaged to begin with. As he'd promised, though, he finished with good news: "You are going to pull out of this."

He warned me my recovery wouldn't be immediate, but everything he saw told him that, ultimately, I would be okay. As the second year of this new life started, I knew I was coming out of whatever it was. I started to feel better, and was finally able to start walking again, then to walk Sparky, and then to get back in shape.

For some reason, I had hit rock bottom once more, and again, instead of my life ending, I was coming back up to the surface. When my strength had completely returned, I reentered the workforce. Ever since that five-and-one-half-year period of lightning bolts, I've been fine. Things aren't always perfect, to say the least, but nothing like these two episodes has occurred.

Unlike my burn recovery, I didn't have much I could do physically to help myself. This time, to keep myself from falling apart emotionally, I had to rely on what I'd learned earlier: all battles are ultimately won or lost by the mind-set you adopt. I'd won before, and I'd win again.

Chapter Twelve

YOU CAN
STILL WIN

For the first year that I struggled with this unknown neuromuscular condition, no one thought I would make it. There could have been a Jeff Kuhn disease, a terminal neuromuscular disorder named after me. As I'm sure Lou Gehrig would say, no one wants to have a terrible illness named after them, but that was the way I was headed.

My situation was different from what had happened after the fire, but it still felt like it was all happening again. It was a totally different curveball, but the result was supposed to be the same: it would end with me dying. I wasn't angry or upset—I just couldn't believe it. After everything I had been through, after everything I had done and so many other people had done to help, I would be gone soon. I couldn't believe Blue Sky Lightning could strike the same person twice, especially not in such a short time span.

The two lightning bolts were within the blink of an eye of each other. I was being told I was going to die again, and this time, it would be a protracted, painful exit, and no one knew what to do about it. Even as I tried to take that in, the humorous side of me was thinking, *If somebody wrote this or put it in a movie, no one would believe it. That I survived the first time seems kind of far-fetched to begin with, and now I'm facing death again? Who would be gullible enough to believe a story like that?*

MY ROADMAPS

Since I had already been on death's doorstep once, I had some stored roadmaps to work with. One of the things I let guide me was building myself back to health. Once the pain was gone, I knew exactly how to get my body back to its full weight and health. As I got better, I did more and more to rebuild my body. Sparky and I went through the recovery together again, and I was finally the person I had been after my first recovery.

The most important roadmap I had, though, was the fact I had already experienced what it's like to be told you really don't have much of a chance. After the burn accident, I had hung on, and it had worked. Now I had a little bit of miniscule hope, and I would hang on to that, too.

I called my condition "the invisible adversary," because no one knew what it was. It had come upon me undetected and had blindsided me with its impact. The doctors had essentially told me this thing would kill me. There was something I never told them, though—on the inside, I kept thinking, *I had last rites and am still standing. I'm not supposed to die yet.*

I focused on the fact they couldn't put a name on what I had. I took that small bit of hope and ran with it. The doctors must have thought this was a nightmare for me. It certainly seemed to scare many of them. There were really difficult aspects to this unknowingness, like not being able to get pain medication, since no one knew what had to be targeted. But not being able to pinpoint exactly what was wrong with me actually worked in my favor. If they couldn't put a name on it, to me it meant there was some hope. The doctors were giving me their best guesses, but their guesses might be wrong. Sometimes not knowing is just what you need to pull through.

HOLDING ON TO HOPE

I've said before that sometimes hope is all you've got. That was the case this time. As I faced my invisible adversary, I thought, *I've been through this before.*

Even though each day was long and painful, I told myself there was no reason for me to mentally check out, because there was always the possibility this would go away. I clung on to the small chance I had. I crossed each day's bridge. I hung on to my shred of hope and worked with it, just as I had when I had been unconscious after my burn accident.

There I was again, with the same amount of limited, minuscule hope—but it had worked before, so why couldn't it work now? When I fought the pain, I would think, *These aren't my last few days. This pain is going to eventually go away, and I'm going to be fine.* That would help me get through each day.

My hope proved correct when my new neurologist decided to do a muscle/nerve biopsy and concluded my nerves and muscles were coming back. When he told me I was going to pull through, hope sprung eternal again.

Like I've said before, you don't need much hope. Even the tiniest shred is enough to hang on to.

MOVING FORWARD...AGAIN

As the pain gradually subsided, and I was able to start exercising again, I did have some muscle and nerve twitches now and then. I was told these might stay with me the rest of my life, but, since they didn't cause any pain, they were something I could live with. I'd learned to be grateful for what I had. Amazingly, though, the twitches eventually went away, too.

You carry the scars from a burn with you forever, but this neuromuscular illness healed completely and left no damage anywhere. It's a blessing to have no lasting remnants or daily nuisances from having gone through it. Still, it's strange to think there is no trace of that illness or those difficult years following my second lightning strike.

Hope is part of what saved me, but I know you can't "hope" your way out of every situation. I happened to have two conditions where the hope was small, but not completely unreasonable. If I had been diagnosed with Lou Gehrig's disease, I could have hoped all I wanted, but I still would have died. If you're in a situation where there's even an extremely small amount of hope, be grateful it's there—hope is a very powerful thing, and a necessary thing. With my two medical ordeals, the hope had to be backed up by an enormous amount of mental and physical firepower.

That said, most of our bad situations aren't terminal or even medical. You could be dealing with the loss of a job or a loved one. In these cases, there is still hope you'll overcome it. One of the amazing things about hope is that a small amount can be just as powerful as a lot. If there is any—and there could be, even if it's just a small amount—hang on to it. Use even that little bit of it to your advantage. Know that you are going to pull through, because there is always that possibility.

YOUR POWER

This book is not about how to survive and pull out of horrendous medical calamities. You don't go through life unscathed. We're all going to experience times that are difficult. Your situation is totally unique, but in some ways, there will be parallels between what you and I have gone through. Hopefully, some of the lessons I learned and some of the mental techniques I used to deal with and overcome the challenges I faced can be of value and help give you motivation, inspiration, and encouragement to hang on yourself and get to a new, better place.

I'll never stop being impressed by the desire that's hardwired into all of us to live, fight, and carry on. Everyone has this strength within them. They can summon it forward when it's necessary to put up a fight, whatever the fight might be.

I think most people underestimate how strong they are, until something unfortunate happens to them. Then the will to survive and carry on comes out. You may not believe you have it—I didn't know I had it in me. If someone had told me what I would live through during those five years, I wouldn't have believed them.

You will face difficult times in your life. Hopefully, they won't be as dramatic as mine, but they will come. Don't worry, because you have a strong fight within you. We all have such immense strength. As I write this, even my parents, who are in their nineties, fight every day and don't give up. And you won't either.

Chapter Thirteen

———

WHEN YOU FINALLY MOVE BEYOND THE CATASTROPHE

Two years after my inexplicable neuromuscular condition hit, the pain was gone and my health and muscle mass had returned. I had survived two catastrophes in roughly five-and-a-half years, and now I was ready (again) to live a normal life.

I'd been sending out résumés nearly every day for six months and was becoming dismayed at the lack of responses. One day, I was out walking Sparky when I looked up at the sky and said, "I have dreams, too." It was like I was speaking to the universe, telling it, "A lot's been thrown at me, and I've taken it. Here I am, ready to move on."

Within the next couple of weeks, I got a call from a top real estate developer in Phoenix, Arizona, where I'd applied for a job. May 1, 1995, would be my first day.

I had just enough time to move there and get my real estate license, but I didn't feel panicked—I felt great. The minute you have a job offer, you can rent a house. Now I had a small house in Phoenix with a pool. I had gone through two life-threatening situations and two long recoveries, and now I had a job and my own home. I had been broke, and now I was going to get a paycheck. I was even able to buy a new car, a Toyota 4Runner that Sparky loved to ride in.

The new job suited me. I had great coworkers and bosses. I was happy living the life I had wanted for so long and saving money. Now that I was healthy and in a stable situation, I realized I could actually ask someone out on a date.

SCARS AND ACCEPTANCE

Imagine it—you're single and you haven't been on a date in over two years. You're also covered in scar tissue. Suddenly, I was meeting women and thinking I could ask them out. It was an amazing feeling.

I did worry about my scars and skin grafts, of course.

Would women be turned off or even repulsed by them? I wouldn't blame them if they were. Most people probably hadn't seen anything like it.

At least I was fortunate when it came to my face. It had been covered in second-degree burns, but I was very lucky it had healed so well. Dr. Rohrich had reconstructed my scalp (which had sustained a large third-degree burn) so my hairline and hair looked the same. When I'm dressed, if I tell someone what happened to me, they find it hard to believe I was injured so badly. Still, I do have plenty of scars. They just aren't in places people can see.

My doctors and I had worked hard to minimize these scars. For over two years, I wore a burn compression suit, which kept the scarring from "bubbling up." Without constant pressure, I could have developed keloid scars, which are large, raised (and unsightly) scars. Most burn patients use pressure garments when they're healing. In my case, because I had been burned almost everywhere, my suit covered my entire body below the neck. I would wear the suit underneath my clothes, even under my shirt and coat when I was selling cars. Let me tell you, it gets pretty toasty in a Dallas used car lot, even without a compression suit.

But the discomfort had been worth it. Now I looked about as good as a person who had been injured as much as I had possibly could. But I still didn't know what to expect.

Luckily, as I've said before, I haven't met a single person who has felt repulsed or turned off by my scars and skin grafts. In fact, whether it was someone meeting me when I was in a bathing suit or a woman I was on a date with, I would explain why I had them, giving a much shorter version of what you've read here, of course. The only response I ever got was, essentially, "I'm so sorry you had to go through all that."

I've said before how good this makes me feel about human nature. I've found people really do believe that beauty is more than skin deep. They like me for who I am as a person, regardless of how I look. My scars—or, as I like to call them, my "battle scars"—don't bother them at all, just as they don't bother me. It's turned out that when people see them, they see I've been through a lot, and, in a way, I'm a warrior.

My return to dating had started off even better than I could have expected. I found myself having fun and wondering who I was going to meet. Would I ever have a family?

A HAPPY GUY

So much had been taken away from me over the previous five years. Now, I had a brand-new start. When I think about how that felt, I still get excited about it today. I had a good, steady job I liked and a bank account with money I had earned. I had my own place and my own car. I was able to support and take care of Sparky and myself again. It was amazing to finally have reached this place, and I didn't take a single moment for granted.

At work, people were impressed I was always in a good mood and laughing. Most of them had no idea what I had been through; they must have thought I was just a happy guy.

BECOMING A DAD

One night a few years later, in June 2001, my son was born. I remember holding him for the first time around three in the morning. He grabbed my index finger with his tiny hand. As he squeezed, I couldn't believe how strong he was. I looked down at him, smiling, and the first thing I said to him was, "I have a new best friend." And he has been.

That was the happiest day of my life.

Despite everything I had been through, I helped bring a new life into the world. I couldn't help thinking about the question my mom had asked the doctors the day of my burn accident.

"Let's assume he makes it. Can he have children?"

The odds of me ever being in that hospital room with my wife and child were so far beyond the realm of possibility, but there I was. When my life had been so close to being taken from me, one of the things that had kept me going was the dream of being married and having a kid someday, and there he was. Sometimes, I look at pictures of myself with my son when he was little, the two of us wrestling on the ground with our dogs, and I think, *That's what the fight was all about.*

Having a child does change your life. One minute, it's just you and your wife, and the next, you've got a kid to take care of. You have to think of so many details—diapers, who will watch him, where he will go to school. A few billion new concerns come into your life, but it's all wonderful. My son is a teenager now, about to go to college. We raised a great kid.

If someone asked me what the best part of being alive is, I'd say owning a dog is second only to being a father in a loving relationship. That's my greatest joy. All of the pain and suffering, the surgeries and nightmares I went through were worth it, and then some, just to have the opportunity to be a dad and have the life I've had.

THE PURPOSE IN THE PAIN

In the difficult years I spent dealing with those two lightning bolts, I tried not to ask "Why me?" I've always felt this is a really easy trap to fall into. When bad things happen, if you make yourself feel you've been singled out by the cosmos and start asking "Why me?" all that's going to do is lead to depression. It won't result in anything productive. I coped by honestly believing: better me than anyone else. I wouldn't wish what happened to me on any human being—even my worst enemy.

I don't fully understand why I went through these two traumatic events. For a while, I thought maybe my life had been spared because I would go on to do something incredibly positive for humanity.

Well, twenty-five or so years have gone by, and I've realized that's probably not it. As I said, I'm okay with what happened to me, because I'd rather it be me than anyone else. But I did still search for answers about why it happened. I came to the conclusion I survived so I could have a son. Maybe *he's* going to go on to do something great for humanity. I may not live long enough to see it, but maybe that's it.

Then, a little more time passed, and the idea of writing a book about what I went through came to me. Now I think maybe there's even more to the purpose of going through those two calamities: so I can tell other people about it.

I believe I went through what I did so I could share it and

help other people as they battle with their own troubles. I hope this will happen. If my story can give even one person the strength, inspiration, or courage to carry on until they get to a better place, then what I went through will have been worth it.

Chapter Fourteen

———

YOUR STORY
MATTERS

One day in December 2017, I wrote an article about my experiences and posted it on LinkedIn. I hadn't really thought about it—I just wrote it all down and put it out there. Then, to my surprise, about a thousand people read it. Although I tend to look at things mathematically, that number didn't matter to me. What did matter was the feedback I got and continue to get.

People reached out to me, sharing their own stories. They weren't all necessarily burn victims. Some of them had experienced things like domestic abuse, loss, other kinds of trauma. What they wrote moved and inspired me, and made me realize the lessons I learned—about hope, about taking it day by day, about not being alone, about never giving up—apply far beyond any burn unit. I loved reading what they had to say and feeling the connection that had been created between us. Everyone has struggles in life, and we feel as if we're alone. But I realized when you share your story, you show others this isn't true. We're not alone.

People told me how my story spoke to them or even that it had given them the courage to go on another day. The thing is, their stories inspired *me*. They should be writing a book.

Some of those who contacted me weren't going through struggles right now, themselves, but found my story helpful when it came to relating to people in their lives who were. A few doctors in fields like cancer and plastic surgery have gotten in touch to say they appreciated reading about the things I went through from a patient's perspective.

These reactions are part of what inspired me to write this book. The point of it isn't to tell my story or pat myself on the back for surviving two near-death experiences. It's about connecting with and helping each other through our challenges. I also hope it will inspire people to share their own stories with as many other people as possible. Your story matters, and it can help someone.

SHARING YOUR PROBLEMS

You may not believe anyone will want to listen to your problems. It's true that when bad things happen, even the people you thought would stick around may not. Everyone has their own lives and their own struggles, so why do they want to think about yours on top of theirs?

You might wonder whom you could talk to even if you wanted to, besides someone like a doctor or physical therapist. Whatever your issues, when you leave the world of professional help and return to a mainstream environment, you think, *Everyone has their own stuff going on. Who wants to hear about mine?*

You might also feel like your story is worth telling, but you don't think anyone will really get it. This can be especially true for people like me, who have gone through a traumatic event like a burn injury. The length of time it would take for me to explain something like the "baths" in the burn unit may make some people just tune out. Even if they do listen and care, they might not truly understand the pain I experienced or what it took to recover from that type of injury—or from a neuromuscular illness, for that matter. It seems easier to stay silent.

Another thing that may make you feel that telling your story isn't worth it is your own brain trying to protect you. Sharing your experiences means you have to relive the bad things you went through, as well as the good, and that may not be something you really want to do. Whatever traumatic incident you've been through, humans have a natural defense mechanism that makes us feel like it's better to just wall it up, suppress it, and go about our business.

To some extent, this defense mechanism by the brain is a good thing. Even doctors seem to think so. A few years after my injury, I wanted to volunteer at the burn unit, but the staff wouldn't let me. When I insisted, they said, "Look, you went through something really traumatic. You remember nice parts of it, like the kind people you met, but if you come back and volunteer here, *all* of the memories are going to come flooding back, including a lot of bad stuff that you probably don't remember and that your brain is protecting you from."

I think fear makes a lot of people clam up and not want to share their stories. But they should. In fact, taking your experiences out into the world might not just help you—it can help others as well.

THE IMPORTANCE OF SHARING—WHEN YOU'RE READY

I had a deep desire to help other people who were going through what I had, but despite what I believed, I wasn't the perfect guy to do it. I didn't belong in a burn unit. Whatever positive things I had gotten out of my time there would be wiped away when I started to see people suffering. They told me to volunteer somewhere else instead.

Of course, you have to be ready to share your experiences in the first place. For many years, I found it was very hard for me to talk about mine, especially immediately after. I just wanted to move on from it.

My wife, Gail, told me that when we met, just two years after I'd recovered from my neuromuscular disease, I would only give short explanations to people we met; otherwise, I avoided talking about what had happened to me. If people asked questions, I would be friendly, but I'd tell them, "You know, I really don't want to go there," and, of course, they would let it go. Because of this, my wife never really learned a lot of details about these fights for my life, either. I think when she reads this book, she'll probably be surprised by a lot of it. It was just too hard for me to talk about, for a very long time.

Now, more than twenty-five years have gone by, and I have a new outlook and sense of purpose. I've had time to reflect and heal, and I know my story, like anyone's, can help other people.

When you're ready, share your story, too. Whether you

write and publish something like I have, or you sit down with the right person and talk about it, some good will come from releasing it, even if you have to touch on some sad memories. There is a true relief from talking about something hard you've been through.

YOUR STORY CAN HELP OTHERS

There is, of course, another huge benefit to sharing your story I've been getting at: it might help someone else.

This is something I've slowly realized. For so many years, I was solely focused on returning to a normal life. Now that my son is getting older and heading to college, I've started to wonder what my purpose will be.

My personal physician, Dr. Melissa Levine, told me, "Get a life." She's been my doctor for about twenty years and was just giving me some "tough love."

It was an epiphany.

I've always wanted to help people, especially after all the help I was given during those hard years. Now I realized my story is so extreme that by telling it, I might be able to give something back.

There are lots of people out there who are suffering in

silence. Maybe if they read my story, they will think, *It has to be hard for this guy to go deep and relive this whole thing. If he can talk about what he went through, maybe I can, too.* I want to reach so many people, especially those who don't know whom to turn to, or who think they're alone.

When I published my LinkedIn article, many of the people who got in touch with me would only open up to someone who they thought really got what they were going through, and who had been through trauma as well. I hope for those who haven't reached out, and won't, they'll at least read my story and know that if I can make it, they can, too. Giving up crosses everyone's mind, but it's not an acceptable solution.

I'LL SAY IT AGAIN—YOU'RE NOT ALONE

You might think what you're going through is so unique that no one else could possibly understand it. Even though this planet has more than seven billion people living on it, you could be telling yourself, "I'm probably the only one who's ever been through this, so what's the point of talking about it?"

In reality, a lot of us are going through almost the same thing, even if our stories aren't exactly mirrors of one another. We may never meet in person, but all of us who have struggled and who are struggling are fighting together, arm in arm. You might not have been burned as I was, but I bet there are parts of my struggle that resonate with you. That's because when it comes down to it, fighting a battle is fighting a battle, and it's something we can all identify with. We're all in this together. I'm telling you that if you're struggling right now, my heart is with you. I care. And so do many others who would hear your story.

You are not alone.

If you're still not convinced, there's another way to look at it. You never know who might resonate with your unique experience. Maybe your story will bring comfort and motivation to someone who hasn't found it anywhere else.

THE EXTRA PUSH

Trust the process. Don't give up, and when you're ready, give back by telling your story.

I know the pain and length of the ordeal you're going through, the mental and physical strain. It's like running a marathon with a hundred pounds strapped to your back—almost impossible, but still doable.

No matter how bad you think things are, keep putting up that incredible fight for a better future. Keep pushing on, because that better future is just ahead of you. Maybe reading this book, or discovering someone else's story, will give you that extra push to the brighter tomorrow that's waiting for you.

CONCLUSION

This book isn't meant to be a Jeff Kuhn autobiography. My goal isn't to earn any kind of admiration for what I went through.

I've written it because I want to encourage people to fight their battles and make it through. I want people to know there is always hope and the fight is always worth it. And, of course, if nothing else, I hope reading my story will help people who are struggling know they are not alone.

I also hope that by reading my story, more people might begin to share theirs.

Sometimes we don't want to talk about things we've gone through for reasons I've mentioned earlier. But I'm here to tell you there is great power in sharing your story, once you're ready.

THE BEST PART OF SHARING MY STORY: OTHER STORIES

After I wrote my article on LinkedIn, I heard from people around the world. I heard from doctors who had gained insight into their patients' experiences and people who are in the middle of a struggle similar to mine. I even heard from people who were in a completely different kind of struggle, but who read about me overcoming mine and found the strength to continue to fight their own.

Some of them would tell me I was an inspiration, and I'd write back to tell them *they* are an inspiration to *me*. Their stories were incredible, and I admired their bravery.

Writing that article was cathartic and healthy for me, but the best part ended up being hearing from other people and knowing my story has affected them in a positive way. Whenever someone writes to tell me what I wrote has helped them with what they're going through or what they've been through, I genuinely get excited. I feel such great joy in knowing what I shared meant something to them.

I know now, after hearing from so many people, that there are so many stories, so much inspiration out there beyond what I have to offer. And so I hope my story will encourage others to reach out and share their own struggles and inspiring stories.

THE POWER OF SHARING

I think all of our stories together could provide so much inspiration and encouragement for other people. That includes me.

My life isn't over. Just because I've overcome some major struggles doesn't mean I'm not going to have any more. I want to hear how you are fighting, or how you have fought your battles, because I gain encouragement and inspiration from others. If I run into more hurdles in my life—and I'm sure I will—I can use your encouraging stories to help me.

One story I often think about is a man who reached out to me after he read my LinkedIn article. He told me the story of how he became a fireman after his two daughters died in a house fire. Becoming a firefighter, he said, was the only way he could cope with the overwhelming sadness of losing his only children. This man is an inspiration to me. If I run into troubles, I'll be thinking about him and how he made it through. If I can share stories like his with other people and help them, too, that's even better.

BE AN INSPIRATION

So, please tell me your story.

You can reach me at Twitter: @jmkuhn99, or you can

contact me on LinkedIn: https://www.linkedin.com/
in/jeffreymkuhn/. I am listed as Jeff Kuhn, MBA, in Los
Angeles, California. I'm hopeful that each person who
does reach out will inspire someone else to do the same.
It will create a domino effect that will lead to an incredible, inspiring resource for anyone out there who is going
through a tough time, no matter how impossible overcoming their struggles may seem.

If you think I'm an inspiration, well, thank you. But I
believe if you are reading this, *you* are an inspiration,
even if you don't see yourself that way. Your story has
more power than you realize. When you're ready, share
it with the world and help someone else realize no one
is really alone.

EPILOGUE: SPARKY AND ME

Sparky was born in on January 8, 1988, in McKinney, Texas, a year and a half before the fire. She was seven by the time I recovered from my neuromuscular disease. She was my first dog, the one I'd planned on having since I was a kid. She was there for me during my worst times and, later, my best. She took care of me, and I took care of her. She saw the vet every six months. The thing you don't think about when you get a dog is when you'll have to say goodbye.

Sparky lived to be fifteen-and-a-half and passed away from natural causes in April of 2013. Most dogs, when they get to a certain age, have to be put to sleep. Every other dog I've owned since had to be put to sleep. Sparky is the only one that actually made it all the way and just passed away on her own.

The night Sparky died, my wife, Gail, my son, JT, and I were living in Hermosa Beach, California, after I'd gotten a job there in mortgage banking. We had just closed on a new house. Life was good. A friend of mine had just bought a townhome nearby and was having a housewarming party on a Saturday night. We drove out to attend.

When we came home that night, it was late, probably around midnight. JT had a sitter. Sparky was in the backyard, just unresponsive.

Our vet, Emily, whom I'd become very close with over the years had tried to warn me. "Jeff, we really need to talk," she'd said to me during one visit. She was trying to tell me the end was near for Sparky. I wouldn't even listen.

"Sparky is fine," I told her. I drove Sparky home that day in my 4Runner. "Sparky, you're fine," I told her, while she sat in the rear of the SUV—smiling as always.

Mentally, I just couldn't face the reality of it. Maybe that sounds strange. I faced my own all but certain death twice, head-on, but the thought of losing Sparky—that was just too much.

"Nothing is going to happen to this dog," I told myself. I was in complete denial.

When we came home that Saturday night and found her unresponsive in the backyard, the truth hit me. She was gone. I just lay down right there on the grass beside her and hugged her.

For over an hour and a half, I just cried into her fur while my wife was on the phone. We didn't know what to do. It was already late in the night on a Saturday. Whom do you call? I told her to call Emily, but, inside, I knew we were past any help she could offer.

Somebody came and got her, but for that hour and a half, I did not let go of her, and just cried and cried and cried. I was so upset I had to take the next three days off from my job. I just couldn't work. I was devastated.

We had another dog at that point, Laddie. We had adopted him when we were in Tucson, and he was about three or four at that time. Having Laddie around was a big help. Like Sparky had been, he was there to help us through a tough time. There's something special about having a dog to get you through the loss of another dog. Still, Sparky was so special to me, the blow of her loss was devastating. She had been through so much with me. After my three days off, I pulled myself together enough to go back to work. I thought, *Look, she lived fifteen-and-a-half years. That's a long time.* I got over it. But I still think about her every day. There are pictures of her all over the house. She will always live in my heart.

Sparky was the only dog I ever bought from a breeder. My wife and I adopted Laddie from a shelter. From then on, we've adopted all our dogs. We got Marley at the shelter. We got Tessie at the shelter. We got PC at the shelter. We've gotten Cheeto and Zoey, our cats, from the shelter as well. It was a way of helping animals that needed loving homes.

My son, JT, loves animals like I do. When he got old enough, we began to volunteer at the Humane Society together. We were trained to work with dogs and cats, and we go to adoption events where we walk dogs around that have "Adopt Me" signs around their necks. It's really fun. I feel the time we spend with shelter animals is part of Sparky's legacy. That love for animals—the ones we've adopted and the ones we've helped find homes—is inspired by what she gave us.

Still, there was only one Sparky, and I'll be forever grateful for the support and unconditional love she gave me along the way. As part of my grieving process, I once wrote her a letter. I know it might seem odd to write a letter to a dog, especially one that's passed, but I needed to express these things somehow, and so I wrote them down.

The letter read:

To my One True Friend—Sparky,

You've been there through it all with me. When others turned their backs and left me you stood by my side. When my career and finances were destroyed you did not leave. When I was hurt or crying or in severe pain, you did not betray me. You were loyal and faithful and took the place of my best friend while others headed for greener pastures. Through all the good times and bad, you have been my one true friend. I love you as much as any man could love an animal. You are one of God's finest creations. I've tried to be your best friend, too.

Until we meet again...

ABOUT THE
AUTHOR

JEFF KUHN is a survivor of severe burns and a rare, unknown neuromuscular disease. After receiving massive attention for his LinkedIn article, "It's Hard to Beat Someone Who Never Gives Up," detailing his struggles with recovery, he decided to share his story further with his book, Blue Sky Lightning. Jeff lives with his wife and son in Los Angeles, California, where he volunteers at a local animal shelter. You can learn more about him and share your own stories of survival at his LinkedIn website: https://www.linkedin.com/in/jeffreymkuhn/. Or, you can reach him via Twitter @jmkuhn99.